MIX*ING*
MES**SAGES**

MIX*ing*
MES**SAGES**

CONTEMPORARY GRAPHIC DESIGN IN AMERICA

ELLEN LUPTON

COOPER-HEWITT

NATIONAL DESIGN MUSEUM

SMITHSONIAN INSTITUTION

AND

THAMES AND HUDSON LTD

First Published in Great Britain in 1996
by Thames & Hudson Ltd, London

Published concurrently in the United States by
Princeton Architectural Press, New York

British Library Cataloguing-in-Publication Data

A catalogue record for this book is available from
the British Library

ISBN 0-500-27923-3

Printed in Canada

The exhibition
*Mixing Messages:
Graphic Design in Contemporary Culture*
has been made possible by
The Mead Corporation.

Technology sponsored by Microsoft.

Additional support provided by
Smithsonian Institution Special Exhibition Fund
National Endowment for the Arts, Design Arts Program
and Duggal Color Projects.

CONTENTS

KEEP THE
IRREGULARITIES INCONSISTENT,
VARIOUSLY DIFFERENTIATED,
AND ✭OTHERWISE UNMATCHED
IN ALL MANNER OF WAYS
AND VARIETY OF SORTS.

'DEED I DO.

SO, SO.

DESIGNED FOR AND BY : THE ABOVE

Design Department
CRANBROOK ACADEMY of ART (and DESIGN)
P.O. Box 801
Bloomfield Hills, MICHIGAN 48303-0801

NON-PROFIT
ORGANIZATION
U.S. Postage
PAID
PERMIT NO 5
Bloomfield Hills MI

Keep the Irregularities Inconsistent
Poster, 1993, offset lithograph
Designer and publisher:
Edward Fella (b. 1938), Los Angeles
For the Design Program, Cranbrook
Academy of Art and Design
Collection Cooper-Hewitt, National Design
Museum, Gift of the designer

ACKNOWLEDGMENTS

This book was published in conjunction with the exhibition *Mixing Messages: Graphic Design in Contemporary Culture,* organized by Cooper-Hewitt, National Design Museum. The exhibition was made possible by The Mead Corporation. I am grateful to numerous individuals and divisions at Mead, including Marty Hydell and Julie Busse, Mead Coated Papers; Stacey Rimassa and Kathy Merckx, Gilbert Paper; Su McLoughlin, Mead Coated Board; and Kathy Strawn and the Mead Corporation Foundation. Above all, I am indebted to Hilary Strauss, Mead Coated Papers, who championed the project from its inception and was a key collaborator throughout the design process.

The Microsoft Corporation sponsored a series of multimedia installations created for the exhibition. I am grateful for the advocacy and creativity of Toni Jennings, Denise Shephard, and Linda Stone at Microsoft, who worked hard to bring the exhibition into the electronic realm.

The project was awarded a grant by the Smithsonian Institution's Special Exhibition Fund, which allowed us to initiate our research on contemporary graphic design. Additional support was provided by Duggal Color Projects, New York. Baldev Duggal and Glenn Rabbach provided crucial assistance with the design and production of graphics for the exhibition.

Many designers and scholars made key contributions to the project. Sheila Kennedy, Frano Violich, Markus Froehlin, and James Moore of Kennedy & Violich Architecture designed the exhibition. Their efforts yielded an environment that critically and creatively converses with the historic fabric of the Carnegie Mansion.

A display of large-scale three-dimensional letters was fabricated courtesy of Kaltech Industries; I am grateful to Eric Silverstein and Mustak Khalfan for their support. Chris Calori designed the installation of the letters, and Juanita Dugdale provided research services.

The typography of the font room was designed by Frederick Gates.

A special installation on view at the American Institute of Graphic Arts, *Design on the Street: Mixing Messages in Public Space,* was designed and curated by Eva Christina Kraus. Research was directed by Paul Makovsky. This special installation was made possible by a grant from the Design Arts Program of the National Endowment for the Arts.

An electronic installation on the future of publishing and an anthology of CD-ROM publications were designed by Jessica Helfand with Peter Girardi. Elisabeth Roxby designed a site on the World Wide Web that brings the project to a global audience. A video on typography and the moving image was designed by Emily Oberman and Bonnie Siegler.

A team of outside advisors responded to the concept of the exhibition in its earliest planning phase and continued to add insights and ideas; I thank Steven Heller, Natalia Illyin, Rebeca Méndez, David Peters, Michael Rock, and Sylvia Harris.

The book and exhibition could not exist without the talented group of designers whose work the project celebrates. I am grateful to all the designers who contributed artifacts and participated in their documentation and interpretation.

An exhibition is a vast undertaking that involves every department of a museum, from the security force to curators, registrars, and conservators.

The Department of Drawings and Prints and the Library made the exhibition possible by launching a major collecting initiative. During the course of producing the book and exhibition, the Museum collected and documented over fifteen hundred examples of contemporary design. I am especially indebted to Gail Davidson, Alison Eisendrath, Samantha Finch, India Leval, Liz Marcus, Beth Petriello, John Randall, Scott Ruby, Marilyn Symmes, Allison Unruh, and Stephen van Dyk.

The Design Department brought concrete, physical form to the exhibition and its related publications; I thank Christine McKee, Jennifer Roos, Brent Rumage, and Mathew Weaver. I also thank the Museum's team of professional installers and preparators, including Anne Burton, Craig Hensala, Arvid Johnson, Linda Levinson, Paul Pellegrino, and Raul Serrano. Additional services were provided by Ken Perkins and Charles Golden/Golden Industries.

A team of smart and energetic curatorial assistants worked on the project over the course of its development; I thank Brett MacFadden, Mary Martone, Timothy McCormick, Sheri Sandler, Rachel Switzky, and, above all, Paul Makovsky, who directed research on the project from its inception.

The Education Department participated in curatorial meetings and orchestrated an ambitious program of lectures, tours, seminars, and publications. I am especially grateful to Julie Carmelich, Dorothy Dunn, Kerry Macintosh, Mei Mah, Lisa Mazzola, and Egle Zygas.

Several people worked hard to bring the exhibition to public attention and to ensure that it was adequately funded; I thank Pamela Haylock, Laura James, Barbara Livenstein, and Sheri Sandler.

The challenging task of editing texts for the book and exhibition was managed calmly and creatively by Nancy Aakre, Kathleen Luhrs, and Susan Yelavich at the National Design Museum, and by Mark Lamster at Princeton Architectural Press. Maud Lavin graciously served as an outside reader. Thomas Forget assisted with the index.

The entire museum staff contributed to the success of the project. Special thanks goes to Linda Dunne, Lucy Fellowes, Steven Langehough, Heather Lemonedes, Jeff McCartney, Caroline Mortimer, Marla Musick, Luis Palau, Angelo Rodriguez, Cordelia Rose, Larry Silver, Rona Simon, and Hilda Wojack.

My deepest thanks goes to our Director, Dianne H. Pilgrim, who has encouraged me in all of my work since I joined the Museum in 1992, and who embraced this project as a fitting reopening for the galleries after a year of closure for renovation.

I thank my friend, Jennifer Tobias, for her patience, wit, and discipline. My family is always with me, even when they are far away; I thank Mary Jane Lupton and Kenneth Baldwin, William and Shirley Lupton, and Julia Reinhard Lupton and Kenneth Reinhard. My son, Jay Lupton Miller, fills my days with light. Finally, none of my work would be possible without J. Abbott Miller. I thank him with all my heart. **ELLEN LUPTON**

No Surprises
Book, 1990, offset lithograph
Designer: Jilly Simons (b. 1949) with David Robson
Art director: Jilly Simons
Firm: Concrete
Publisher: Ace Lithographers, Chicago
Collection Cooper-Hewitt, National Design Museum,
Gift of Jilly Simons
The random mix of images and texts in this book results from
the process of running press proofs in offset printing. Paper
used for testing the printing plates is used repeatedly. Simons
bound together a series of these pages, called "make ready"
sheets, in this book published by a printing plant.

INTRODUCTION

Between 1980 and 1995 graphic design in the United States took part in revolutionary changes in communications. The rise of desktop computers encouraged the growth of small design studios and the emergence of independent producers of books, magazines, and music. Although this period also witnessed the rise of vast media empires and widespread nostalgia for a world defined by common values, there remained space for numerous voices to be seen and heard. In the field of graphic design, no single aesthetic approach identified this era, which accommodated diverse styles and methods, media and messages, makers and users of visual information.

Cooper-Hewitt, National Design Museum understands design as an *active process* of making and communicating rather than a body of static artifacts. As an active process, graphic design involves forging relationships between images and texts by cutting and pasting, enlarging and reducing, layering and framing, comparing and isolating. Designers use pencils, cameras, scissors, and scanners to generate new images and letterforms or to piece together ready-made elements. Since the rise of mass media in the mid-nineteenth century, graphic arts technologies have promoted the manipulation and collage of existing material. Never has the ability to mix disparate elements been greater than during the past fifteen years. Digital imaging, page layout programs, type design software, and video production technologies have given designers new ways to find, create, manipulate, and disseminate images and information. Graphic design as a process involves the making of visual statements and their use and revision by clients, audiences, and other designers. *Mixing* characterizes the social life of graphic design. Visual communications elicit divergent responses in a crowded landscape of competing messages. The meaning of signs and styles shifts with the context in which they are sent and received. Designers visualize the identities of various institutions and cultural groups, from international corporations and government agencies to clusters of people connected by modes of art, music, politics, or sexuality. The products of graphic design, from commercial trademarks to experimental typefaces, are invested with significance by their initial makers. Once in public circulation, they are subject to change.

What is "graphic design"? How broad is its territory? How deep is its history? Defined historically, graphic design is a profession that took shape in industrialized societies during the twentieth century. This new discipline emerged out of the eruption of mass consumption and the critical avant-gardes. Graphic design also can be defined more inclusively as a category encompassing any form of communication in which signs are scratched, carved, drawn, printed, pasted, projected, or otherwise inscribed onto surfaces. While the narrower historical view describes design as a modern institution grounded in specific traditions and social functions, the wider view accommodates any mode of human communication that employs visible marks, from cave painting to desktop publishing.

In a conversation in June 1994, designer Dan Friedman addressed the dilemma of defining the field: "Is graphic design pervasive throughout society, or is it virtually non-existent?" On the one hand, design is utterly commonplace, appearing everywhere and produced by anyone. Its past and future are coterminus with human history. On the other hand, design represents a set of refined and narrow interests within a vast web of communications. Viewed from this perspective, design has a brief history and a fragile future.

This project alternates between these two views. While the more inclusive definition of design appears liberating and democratic at first glance, it can serve to generalize all forms of expression into a value-free flood of signals. In contrast, an overly narrow definition of design can polarize a diverse array of practices into such categories as design/non-design, professional/non-professional, and

mainstream/marginal. These oppositions devalue some practices in relation to others, naming a legitimate center and an ancillary fringe.

Graphic design is a historically specific profession, one that touches and includes various subcultures. The figure of the professional graphic designer emerged in the 1920s and 1930s in Europe, North America, and Asia. The new "design consultant" mediated between clients and production processes, offering expertise on appropriate materials and technologies as well as on appearance and content. The designer generated instructions to be executed by industrial craftspeople. Knowledge of modern aesthetics and theories of functional communication distinguished the new discipline of design from traditional "commercial art," which was provided to businesses directly by printers.

The contemporary profession of graphic design consists of people connected by shared interests—by educational theories and practices, by trade organizations and publications, and by customs of hiring and firing, marketing and billing. The design profession is not a closed, monolithic edifice: it has numerous factions anchored by geography, generation, gender, and education; by commitments to forms of music, sport, fashion, and politics—from snowboarding to AIDS activism.

Some designers view themselves as part of the organized structure of the profession, while others identify more strongly with particular industries or issues. Corporate identity consultants have staked a claim to the center of the profession. Yet even though they bear the discipline's most financially rewarded skills, such experts must still defend the value of their services to the business world. Magazine art directors

A NOTE ON THE CAPTIONS IN THIS BOOK:
Design is a collaborative process. To compile this book, the editorial team attempted to assemble complete credits on all pieces published. Wherever possible, we have provided birth dates for the principle designers on each project.

are bound to the hierarchies and heritage of the publishing industry, and yet also participate in the general community of design professionals. The editors of fanzines or the promoters of independent music labels may deliberately ignore the formal canons of design, being concerned chiefly with the judgment of their peers.

This book is organized around questions of form, function, and medium. Many ideas or individuals introduced in one section reappear in others. The book focuses on the generation of designers who began their careers in the 1980s and early 1990s. Their work is illuminated by the contributions of older designers, whose achievements and philosophies frame current practice.

The book opens with a photo essay that looks at the mix of messages on the street. In urban space, numerous groups and individuals—from political activists to national advertisers—use graphic design to compete for public attention.

The first chapter analyzes design's formal language by looking at *typography*, the art of creating letters for reproduction and organizing them in space. Various theoretical issues animate contemporary practice, from questioning conventional standards of legibility to exploring the relationship between history and modernity.

The following chapter considers the chief social function of design: to visualize the *identity* of institutions and audiences. Museums, schools, businesses, and other institutions express their personalities through logos, signs, and publications. Symbols created for one group can be usurped by another, a process that exploits the familiarity of the original while recasting its meaning. This chapter concludes

by showing how the design profession questioned its own identity during the 1980s and early 1990s.

The final chapter looks at *publishing*. The production and dissemination of books and magazines is a process of making public, of building communities through the exchange of information. The rise of personal computers has overturned traditional publishing methods, changing the role of the designer and spawning hybrid media that mix features of books, magazines, and television.

The first museum exhibition to attempt a broad study of visual communications in the United States was *Graphic Design in America,* curated by Mildred Friedman at the Walker Art Center in 1989. Friedman's ambitious survey, which spanned two centuries of design practice, prepared the ground for *Mixing Messages,* which has attempted to reveal the conflicts that animate a narrower slice of history.

A recurring theme is the friction between the new and the familiar, between construction from ground zero and the quotation of the ready-made. The chapter on typography looks at how designers approach the history of their medium, while the section on identity contrasts the invention of unique signs with the circulation and reuse of visual property. From the printed page to the Internet, publishing constructs the tissue of community, establishing avenues for the exchange of ideas. During the past fifteen years, design has become an increasingly insistent presence in daily life. By looking at graphic design *in* contemporary culture, this book shows how the process of design engages an array of people and artifacts.

Do You Love the Dyke in Your Life?
Poster, 1993, offset lithograph
Designers and publishers: Carrie Moyer (b. 1960)
and Sue Schaffner (b. 1964), New York
Collection Cooper-Hewitt, National Design Museum,
Gift of Carrie Moyer

a fragrance for
a man or a woman

Calvin Klein

Nina, Kate, & Joey, cK one
Outdoor advertisement, 1996, offset lithograph
Creative director: Fabien Baron (b. 1959),
CRK Advertising
Photographer: Steven Meisel
Client: Calvin Klein Cosmetics Company, New York
© 1996 Calvin Klein Cosmetic Corporation

THE STREET

Urban public space is a stage

for viewing the field of graphic design in its diversity.

A mix of voices, from advertising to activism,

compete for visibility.

We Need More Than Magic
Billboard, 1991, offset lithograph
Designer: Gran Fury
Project sponsored by Whitney Museum
of American Art, New York
Photo courtesy Loring McAlpin

Along the road, public and corporate languages mix and overlap.

The theme park and the shopping mall

have become typical urban forms of the late twentieth century.

Warner Bros. Studio Store
Construction sign, 1996, New York
Designers: The Partners, London
Art director: Terron Schaefer
Illustrator: Ron Strang, Superior Backings
Client: Warner Bros. Studio Store,
Burbank/New York
Photographed by Christine McKee

Disney/MGM Studios
Highway sign, 1990
Designers: Deborah Sussman
and Paul Prejza (b. 1939)
Firm: Sussman/Prejza & Co., Inc.
Client: Walt Disney World, Orlando

Traditional urban centers alternate between damaged slums

and preserved historic districts

that are illuminated by interpretive signs.

Municipal Parking
Sign, 1994, New York
Photographed by Mike Mills

Baltimore Waterfront Promenade
Neighborhood marker
maquette, 1992
Designers: David Gibson (b. 1950),
Julie Marable, and Douglas Morris
Firm: Two Twelve Associates
Client: Baltimore Harbor
Endowment

Santa Monica Place
Sign, 1990, Santa Monica
Designer: Communication Arts Inc.
Client: The Rouse Company,
Columbia, Maryland
Photographed by Jerry Butts

Blank walls and construction fences are plastered with a changing mix of messages,

a collage of opinions and promotions.

Bullet Space at Astor Place
Posters, 1991, New York
Photographed by J. Abbott Miller

I Love NY
Poster, 1991, silkscreen
Designer and publisher:
Tom McGlynn (b. 1958), New York
Posted by Bullet Space

Homelessness at Work
Poster, 1991, silkscreen
Designers and publishers:
Day Gleeson (b. 1948) and
Dennis Thomas (b. 1955)
Posted by Bullet Space

Fantera, Sepultura, Prong
Poster, 1994, silkscreen
Designer and publisher:
Lee Bolton (b. 1967), Austin
Collection Cooper-Hewitt, National
Design Museum, Gift of the designer

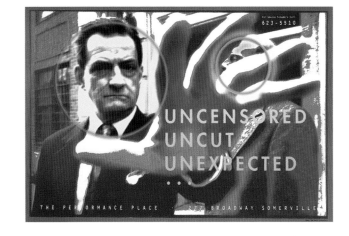

Uncensored, Uncut, Unexpected
Poster, 1992–93, offset lithograph
Designers: Paul Montie (b. 1965)
and Carolyn Montie (b. 1966)
Firm: Fahrenheit

Photography: The Devil's Chauffeur
Publisher: The Performance Place, Boston
Collection Cooper-Hewitt, National
Design Museum, Gift of the designers

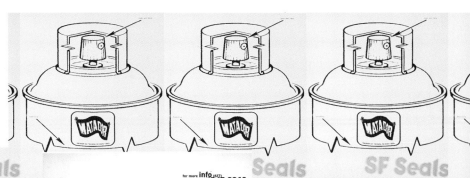

Killdozer
Poster, 1992, silkscreen
Designer: Frank Kozik (b. 1962)
Publisher: ArtRock, San Francisco

Dance Month
Poster, 1994, offset lithograph
Designer: Fritz Klaetke (b. 1966)
Firm: Visual Dialogue
Photographer: William Huber
Publisher: The Dance Complex, Boston
Collection Cooper-Hewitt, National Design Museum,
Gift of the designer

Spray Can
Posters, 1994,
silkscreen
Designer:
Mark Ohe (b. 1958)
Publisher:
Matador Records,
New York
Collection Cooper-
Hewitt, National Design
Museum,
Gift of the designer

Hanks. Gump.
Poster, 1994, offset lithograph
Designer: Robert Tepper (b. 1965)
Creative director: Peter Bemis (b. 1946)
Firm: Frankfurt Balkind Partners
Client: Lucia Ludovico
Studio: Paramount Pictures,
Los Angeles
Photographed by E.G. Camp

Mass cultures and subcultures share space on the stage of the street.

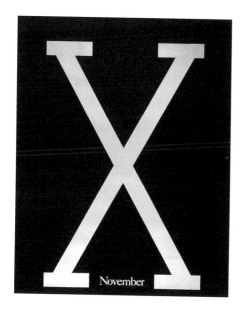

Malcolm X
Poster, 1992, offset lithograph
Designer and art director: Art Sims (b. 1954)
Studio: Warner Brothers, Los Angeles
Collection Cooper-Hewitt, National Design
Museum, Gift of the designer

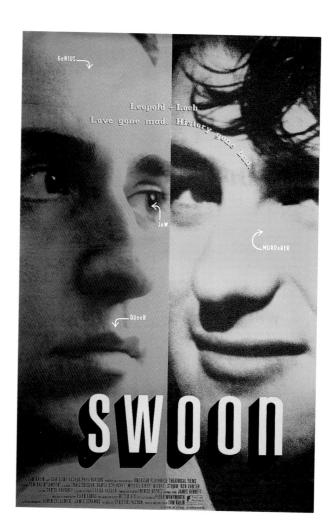

Swoon
Poster, 1992, offset lithograph
Designers: Marlene McCarty (b. 1957)
and Donald Moffett (b. 1955)
Firm: Bureau
Photography: Fine Line Features
Studio: Fine Line Features, New York
Collection Cooper-Hewitt, National Design
Museum, Gift of the designers

New
Poster, 1994, silkscreen
Designer and publisher:
Herbert Hoover (b. 1968), New York
Collection Cooper-Hewitt, National
Design Museum, Gift of the designer

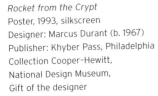

Rocket from the Crypt
Poster, 1993, silkscreen
Designer: Marcus Durant (b. 1967)
Publisher: Khyber Pass, Philadelphia
Collection Cooper-Hewitt,
National Design Museum,
Gift of the designer

Out Let
Poster and invitation, 1994, silkscreen
Designer: Ebon Heath (b. 1972)
Firm: Stereotype
Publisher: Booo Studios, Providence

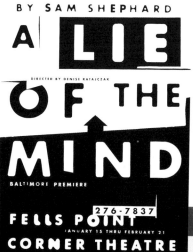

A Lie of the Mind
Poster, 1992, silkscreen
Designers: Paul Sahre (b. 1964)
and David Plunkert (b. 1965)
Publisher: Fells Point Corner
Theater, Baltimore
Collection Cooper-Hewitt, National
Design Museum, Gift of Paul Sahre

The Fever
Poster, 1995, silkscreen
Designer: Paul Sahre (b. 1964)
Publisher: Fells Point Corner
Theater, Baltimore
Collection Cooper-Hewitt, National
Design Museum, Gift of the designer

Man of the Moment
Poster, 1994, offset lithograph
Designers: Robynne Raye (b. 1964)
and Michael Strassburger (b. 1962)
Art director: Robynne Raye
Firm: Modern Dog
Publisher: ACT (A Contemporary Theatre), Seattle
Collection Cooper-Hewitt, National
Design Museum, Gift of the designers

Vagina Envy
Poster, 1994, photocopy, rubber stamp
Designers and publishers:
SisterSerpents, Chicago
Collection Cooper-Hewitt, National
Design Museum, Gift of the designers

Artists and activists use design to aim a message

SOMETHING'S WRONG WHEN FRIGIDAIRE AND WESTINGHOUSE DO A BETTER JOB OF HOUSING THE HOMELESS THAN NEW YORK CITY.

COALITION FOR THE HOMELESS

Camel Jockey
Poster, 1992, offset lithograph
Designers: Steven Brower (b. 1952)
and James Victore (b. 1962) with Post No Bills
Publisher: Post No Bills, New York
Collection Cooper-Hewitt, National
Design Museum, Gift of Steven Brower

Something's Wrong
Poster, 1992, offset lithograph
Designers: Peter Cohen (b. 1955) and Leslie Sweet (b. 1958)
Publisher: Coalition for the Homeless, New York
Collection Cooper-Hewitt, National Design Museum,
Gift of the Coalition for the Homeless

and target an audience.

Republican Contract on America
Poster, 1995, silkscreen
Designer and publisher: Mark Fox (b. 1961)
Firm: BlackDog, San Rafael, California

Time for Prevention
Poster, 1994, offset lithograph
Designer and photographer: Matuschka (b. 1954)
Publisher: Time for Life/Greenpeace
Collection Cooper-Hewitt, National
Design Museum, Gift of the designer

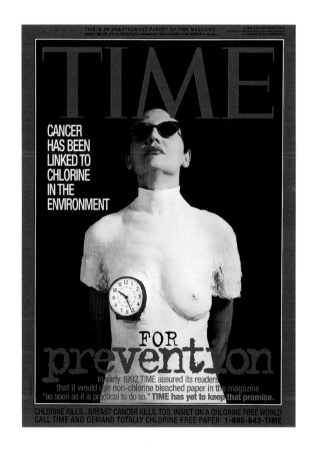

Women's Health Care is Political (c. 1990) and
Breast Cancer: An Epidemic (c. 1992)
Stickers, offset lithograph
Designer and publisher: WHAM! Women's Health
Action and Mobilization, New York
Collection Cooper-Hewitt, National Design Museum,
Gift of WHAM!

I'm with Her
Poster, 1992, diazo print
Designer: Bethany Johns (b. 1956)
Publisher: WAC (Women's Action Coalition), New York,
for 1992 Gay Pride March, Washington, DC

Times Square/NIKE
Outdoor advertisement, 1994,
offset lithograph
Art director: John C. Jay; Creative
director: Dan Wieden; Designer: Petra
Langhammer; Photographer: Stanley Bach

Damn/NIKE
Outdoor advertisement, 1994,
offset lithograph
Art director: John C. Jay; Creative
director: Dan Wieden; Designer: Imin Pao;
Copywriter: Jimmy Smith; Photographer:
John Huet

Garden/NIKE
Outdoor advertisement, 1995,
offset lithograph
Art director: Young Kim; Creative directors:
John C. Jay and Dan Wieden; Copywriter:
Jimmy Smith; Photographer: Exum

LA Seed/NIKE
Billboard, 1995, offset lithograph
Art director: John Jay; Creative director:
Dan Wieden; Designers: Imin Pao and
Nicole Misiti; Photographer: Brad Harris

Advertising agency:
Wieden & Kennedy, Portland, Oregon
Publisher: NIKE, Beaverton, Oregon

THE STREET

See
Bus poster, 1994, offset lithograph
Designers: Robert Wong (b. 1966) and
Andreas Combuchen (b. 1965)
Creative directors: Aubrey Balkind
(b. 1944) and Kent Hunter (b. 1956)
Firm: Frankfurt Balkind Partners
Publisher: Sony Plaza, Inc., New York
Photographed by Kenji Toma

Transit, New Harlem, Malcolm
Gypsy cab cards, offset lithographs
Designers unknown
Collection Camilo José Vergara

Above ground and below ground

the surfaces of mass transit

are mobilized for public address.

Keith Haring at Fun Gallery
Poster, 1983, offset lithograph
Designer: Keith Haring (1958–1990)
Publisher: Fun Gallery, New York
Collection Cooper-Hewitt, National
Design Museum, Gift of the Estate
of Dan Friedman, © The Estate
of Keith Haring

Decision
Subway poster, 1994, offset lithograph
Art director: Jerry Gonzalez
Illustrator: Leon McConnell
Publisher:
New York Department of Health
Collection Cooper-Hewitt, National
Design Museum, Gift of the publisher.
From a series of posters organized
as a pictorial novella that promotes
condom use, abstinence, and mono-
gamy as forms of AIDS prevention. · ▼

Want To Know A Dirty Little Secret?
Subway poster, 1994, silkscreen
Designer and publisher:
Catholic League for Religious and
Civil Rights, New York
Collection Cooper-Hewitt, National
Design Museum, Gift of the publisher

Want To Know a Dirty Little Secret?
CONDOMS DON'T SAVE LIVES.

But restraint does.
Only fools think condoms are foolproof.
Remember, better safe than sorry.

Some common sense and a public service message from the
Catholic League
for Religious and Civil Rights

1011 First Avenue
New York, NY 10022
(212) 371-3191

Public service advertising in subway cars draws on a mix of emotions.

Kustom Kulture
Poster, 1994, offset lithograph
Designer: Art Chantry (b. 1954)
Publisher: Center on Contemporary
Art, Seattle
Collection Cooper-Hewitt, National
Design Museum, Gift of the designer

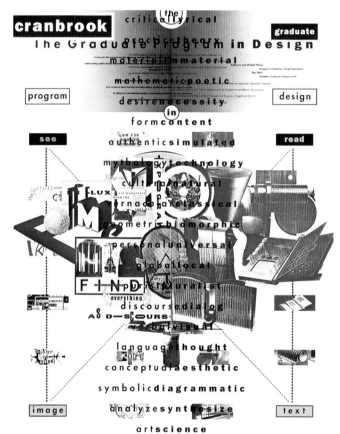

Cranbrook Graduate Program in Design
Poster, 1989, offset lithograph
Designer: Katherine McCoy (b. 1945)
Publisher: Cranbrook Academy of Art,
Bloomfield Hills, Michigan
Collection Cooper-Hewitt, National
Design Museum, Gift of the designer

TYPOGRAPHY

Typography is the design of letterforms and their organization in space. Nearly all visual communications, from books and magazines to film, television, and electronic media, employ typography. Designers use specific styles and arrangements of type in order to attract attention, interpret content, or set a mood. Some typographic forms are so familiar that they recede, becoming a comfortable background for the act of reading; other modes of typographic design attempt to engage the reader by mixing, distorting, and layering letters into unfamiliar patterns. A typeface and the way it is used can declare the identity of an institution, the interests of an audience, or the personal sensibility of a designer. Typography is the basic grammar of graphic design, its common currency. Since the spread of microcomputers and digital communications in the mid-1980s, the makers and users of media in the United States have become increasingly sophisticated about typography. As technologies for generating texts and for mixing words with images have become more powerful and accessible, new fonts and ways to use them have reached an expanding marketplace of typographic consumers, working both inside and outside the design profession. In this increasingly font-conscious culture, typography—a topic once reserved for bibliophiles and trained designers—has entered the realm of popular discourse. Contemporary typography in the United States is an uneven terrain, whose landscape ranges from the austere classicism of the traditional book, to the sensational vocabularies of the mass media, to the technological utopianism of the avant-garde. Over the last twenty years, graphic designers have plumbed the heritage of typographic history, using digital and photographic technologies to generate countless interpretations of typefaces from the near and distant past. This search has broadened the vocabulary of design, while raising questions about appropriate relationships to history. Some designers have sought to base their work in historical or regional traditions, while others have pushed toward new ground. Some have used current technologies to reinvigorate forgotten styles, while others have aimed to invent novel forms for the rapidly unfolding future.

REINVENTING
THE
FAMILIAR

Typography and history have been inextricably linked since the invention of printed letters in the fifteenth century. The written word is the primary medium through which history is recorded, and printing enabled the archives of modern civilization to rapidly expand.[1] Typography can never escape history: every unique aesthetic invention can be absorbed by the past, where it is stored in our memory of reusable styles and structures. While the typographer's art is rooted in the growing body of existing forms, the broader social role of printed letters is to preserve the evidence of civilization in a permanent and tangible form. While some of the most ambitious approaches to graphic design in the twentieth century have sought to reject old traditions in pursuit of originality, typographic forms are always subject to appropriation and reuse—a new typeface quickly enters the public realm, where its meaning is open to change.

Since the Renaissance, the culture of modernity has been fundamentally shaped by technologies of mechanical reproduction, from the printing of texts to the replication of graphic images. As a formal language and a cultural force, typography is at once conservative and revolutionary, working to preserve information while making it accessible to a growing public. The permanence of the printed book has

1. On the origins of typography, see Robin Kinross, *Modern Typography: An Essay in Critical History* (London: Hyphen Press, 1992); and Walter Tracy, *Letters of Credit: A View of Type Design* (Boston: David R. Godine, 1986).

fostered the survival of traditional typefaces and classical page layouts, from decade to decade and century to century.

The rise of mass communications in the nineteenth century countered the conservative functions of typography with the transience of new printed media—advertisements, magazines, newspapers, popular literature. The expanding audiences for print stimulated demand for new typefaces. The introduction of the combined pantograph and router in 1834 revolutionized the production of wood type, used for printing posters and advertisements that required large letters. The pantograph enabled numerous variations to be traced and manufactured from a single base drawing.[2]

The principle of mechanically generating variations of a single letterform remains a prevalent design method today. Cameras have been used throughout the twentieth century to capture existing type specimens to be reissued for new typesetting technologies. In the 1950s, "hot" metal production was replaced with "cold" phototypesetting, in which a film negative is used to expose letters onto light-sensitive paper. Phototypesetting engendered new visual possibilities—the features of handwriting could be easily simulated, and the space between letters could be dramatically reduced.

In the 1970s, a digital signal began to supplant the photographic negative as the means of reproducing typographic forms. In the electronic environment of contemporary type design, scanned alphabets can be endlessly manipulated by the type designer, serving either as models for accurate reproduction or as skeletons for new or hybrid designs.[3]

Variations of Doric Letterforms
Typefaces, 1854
Designers: Wells & Webb
From Rob Roy Kelly, *American Wood Type, 1828-1900*, Van Nostrand Reinhold, New York, 1969.

2. Rob Roy Kelly, *American Wood Type, 1828-1900* (New York: Van Nostrand Reinhold, 1969). See also Nicolete Gray, *A History of Lettering: Creative Experiment and Letter Identity* (Boston: David R. Godine, 1986).

3. On type design and technology, see Darcy DiNucci, "Future Fonts," *Print* 49, 3 (May/June 1995): 28-35; and Matthew Carter, "Typography and Current Technologies," *Design Quarterly* 148 (1990): 56-64.

Bell Centennial
Typeface, design completed 1978
Designer: Matthew Carter (b. 1937)
Produced for Mergenthaler Linotype

TYPOGRAPHY

After the introduction of the Apple Macintosh computer in 1984, and the subsequent development of powerful page-layout software and extensive font libraries, digital typography quickly became the industry norm. PostScript, introduced by Adobe Systems in 1986, allows pages of text and images to be displayed and printed across a broad range of equipment, from video monitors to laser printers to high-resolution imagesetters. PostScript also permits graphic designers to condense, expand, outline, shadow, and slant existing typefaces, a freedom that has enraged guardians of good taste while delighting typographic tinkerers.[4]

The software program Altsys Fontographer, also introduced in 1986, democratized the arcane discipline of originating typefaces. Fontographer and similar programs let type designers immediately proof their work in a variety of sizes and see how letterforms fit together into words and lines, a crucial phase of the design process that once took months or even years to achieve. No longer is type production dominated by large corporate enterprises that can afford the design and manufacturing investment once required to introduce new fonts.

The rise of the Macintosh triggered numerous transformations in the graphic arts. Designers acquired direct control over processes that formerly were divided among typesetters, photo retouchers, paste-up artists, and other specialized technicians. Microcomputers stimulated the proliferation of small design firms and challenged the supremacy of large studios with significant overhead expenses. Around 1984, the term "desktop publishing" entered the English

Dead History, typeface, 1990
Designer: P. Scott Makela (b. 1960)
Courtesy Emigre Fonts, Sacramento

DEAD
HIST
ORY+

32

4. See Philip B. Meggs, "The New Illegibility," *Print* 46, 5 (September/ October 1992): 110-112.
5. *Oxford English Dictionary*. (Oxford: Clarendon Press, 1989).

vocabulary.[5] The early page layout software was daunting for non-professionals, but by 1990, standard word-processing packages contained many of the features found in expert page design programs.[6] Desktop publishing brought typography within the reach of students, office workers, and middle managers, building an appetite for typographic knowledge among the general public.

Alongside the rapid ascendence of desktop publishing there has been a surprising revival of letterpress printing. This Renaissance technology has experienced its own renaissance, reborn as a viable medium for short-run printing and limited-edition publishing. The experimental books of Johanna Drucker and the music packaging of Bruce Licher's Independent Project Press have helped convert an outmoded technology into a contemporary medium. These artists have approached the inherent limitations of letterpress—from the strictly gridded lockups of the type bed to the limited inventory of characters and ornaments in the type case— as a gilded cage, luxurious yet restrictive, from which to compose their curious inventions.[7]

Contemporary type designers have addressed typographic history through faithful restorations and free interpretations of existing alphabets. Adobe Systems has built an extensive library of typefaces for the microcomputer market, working to reissue historical fonts as well as to introduce new styles. The design of Adobe Garamond (1988) combined historical research with contemporary technology. Indeed, the Renaissance typefaces of Claude Garamond have been revived for reproduction by various technologies—from

33

Through Light and the Alphabet
Book, 1986, letterpress
Designer: Johanna Drucker (b. 1952)
Publisher: Druckwerk, Berkeley

Polvo: Celebrate the New Dark Age
Album cover, 1994, letterpress
Designer: Bruce Licher (b. 1958)
Firm: Independent Project Press
Publisher: Merge Records, Chapel Hill
Collection Cooper-Hewitt, National
Design Museum, Gift of the designer

6. Rick Friedman, "Desktop Publishing is No Longer Limited to the Pros," *Office* 112, 1 (July 1990): 14-22.

7. Bruce Licher, interview, *Emigre* 16 (1990). On Johanna Drucker, see Ellen Lupton, "Words Made Flesh," *Eye* 5, 18 (autumn 1995): 72-77.

Adobe Garamond

AaBbCcDdEeFfG
gHhIiJjKkLlMm
NnOoPpQqRrSsTt
UuVvWwXxYyZz

MANTINIA

AABBCCDDEE
FFGGHHIIIJJ
KKLLMMNN
OOPPQQRRSS
TTTUUVVWW
♠XXYY&&ZZ♠

1234567890

metal to digital—during the twentieth century. Each of these revivals was based on sources several generations removed from Garamond's own characters. Designer Robert Slimbach created pencil drawings based on proofs of type cast from Garamond's sixteenth-century molds. He then electronically scanned and redrew the letterforms. Adobe Garamond preserves the humanistic, handmade character of the historic font within the digital realm.[8]

Leading the field of contemporary type design is Matthew Carter, whose career has bridged the transition from large typefoundries to independent producers and from hot metal to photo and digital type technologies. Carter's Bell Centennial (1975), an early example of digital type design, is used today in all United States phone books. Designed for maximum legibility at a minimal size, Bell Centennial has saved millions of trees. Carter's font Walker (1995), created for the Walker Art Center in Minneapolis, aims for expressive flexibility over functional legibility: in Walker, the serifs are separate characters from the main body of the letter; these "snap-ons" come in several styles, allowing the user to mix and match structural elements.

According to Carter, many people who purchase type-faces from Carter & Cone, his Cambridge-based typefoundry, are not design professionals. Their interest was sparked by working on desktop computers. The field of type design also has become more egalitarian: "For most of my life type design has been seen as a brave but arcane business that requires a lifetime's dedication to produce one typeface. I'm happy that notion has gone, that type design has been demystified."[9]

34

The typeface Mantinia, released by Carter & Cone in 1993, is a set of capitals designed to complement Carter's text face Galliard, introduced in 1978. Mantinia includes a range of ligatures—special characters that link two or more letters into a single mark—and other alternative characters that allow the user to fit titles into fixed spaces, rather as a stone cutter pieces together the fabric of a wall. Mantinia is an homage to the fifteenth-century Italian painter Andrea Mantegna, who had studied inscriptions from classical architecture.

Younger type designers include Jonathan Hoefler and Tobias Frere-Jones. They, like Carter, often ground their work in typographic history. Hoefler's revivals include the neo-classical typeface Didot, redesigned for *Harper's Bazaar* in 1992, and the Ziggurat family, created for *Rolling Stone* and based on nineteenth-century advertising letters. Hoefler, whose studio is in New York, describes each of these fonts as an "interpretation that expands upon existing designs without replicating them."[10] Frere-Jones, working at Font Bureau in Cambridge, designed the typeface Interstate in 1993, based on the letterforms used on American highway signs.[11] This book is set in the Interstate family.

While some designers create entire typefaces, the practice of graphic design involves choosing from the vast stock of existing fonts, including historical revivals and recent designs. A typeface has distinctive physical qualities as well as cultural connotations. The individual designer who creates a typeface may endow it with specific intentions. Yet once that font enters the marketplace, it becomes the common property of anyone with access to its forms.

Ziggurat & *Leviathan*
Typefaces, 1993
Designer: Jonathan Hoefler (b. 1970)
Courtesy The Hoefler Type Foundry,
New York

Interstate
Typeface, 1993–94
Designer: Tobias Frere-Jones (b. 1970)
Courtesy Font Bureau, Boston

35

8. Sumner Stone, "The Type Craftsman in the Computer Era," *Print* 43, 2 (March/April 1989): 84-91, 142.

9. Matthew Carter, interview with Erik Spiekermann. *Eye* 3, 11 (winter 1993): 10-16. See also Moira Cullen, "The Space Between the Letters," *Eye* 5, 19 (winter 1995): 70-77;

Dick Coyne, "Matthew Carter," *Communication Arts* 30 (January/February 1989): 86-93; "Type and Technology," *Print* 35,2 (March/April 1981): 29-37; and Robert Bringhurst, "Type in Print: Mantinia and Sophia," *Print* 48, 2 (March/April 1994): 112-13.

10. Jonathan Hoefler, interview with author, New York, June 1994. See also John Belnap, "If the Face Fits," *Eye* 3, 11 (winter 1993): 56-63; and Aileen Rosen, "Hoefler Condensed," *I.D.* (September/October 1994): 94-95.

11. Tobias Frere-Jones, interview with author, Cambridge, November 1995.

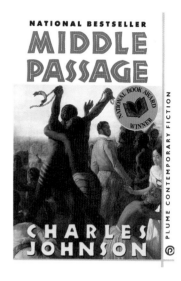

Black Anger
Book cover, 1960, offset lithograph
Designer: Harold Feinstein
Publisher: Grove Press, New York

Marrakesh Express Cous Cous
Package, 1992, offset lithograph
Designer: Robert Horn (b. 1950)
and Allan Butella
Firm: Robert Horn Design Ensemble
Publisher: Melting Pot Foods,
Oak Park, Illinois

July's People
Book cover, 1981, offset lithograph
Designer unknown
Publisher: Penguin Books USA,
New York

Middle Passage
Book cover, 1991, offset lithograph
Designer: Melissa Jacoby (b. 1957)
Publisher: Penguin Books USA, New York

Negro Slave Songs in the United States
Book cover, 1990, offset lithograph
Designer: Morris Taub
Art director: Steven Brower
Publisher: Carol Publishing Group,
New York
Design © Morris Taub, 1990

Consider the historical origins and contemporary uses of the typeface Neuland, designed in Germany by Rudolf Koch in 1923. Translating ideas from Expressionist art into the medium of commercial advertising, Koch designed the rough, heavy forms of Neuland. The letters appear to have been spontaneously carved out of wood rather than carefully cut out of metal. Today, Neuland and letterforms inspired by it frequently are used to signify "Africa." Neuland has appeared, for example, on the covers of numerous books since the early 1960s about the literature and anthropology of Africa and African Americans. The association of Neuland with Africa draws on the font's folk aesthetic, its physical presence, and its dense, bold blackness. The link has become an unstated convention, a form of "stereotypography." Neuland makes one think of Africa because so many publications have used it in that context.

Graphic designers often bank on the familiarity of typefaces to modulate the meaning of their work. The use of existing styles can be clever or banal, serving to reverse expectations or confirm assumptions. The attempt to reinvent the familiar has been a key strategy in American design since the 1940s, when art directors for magazines and advertising mixed abstract, dynamic compositions inspired by European modernism with the ready-made vocabularies of commercial media. A preference for witty concepts based on colloquial idioms over abstract formal solutions marked the graphic design of Saul Bass, Gene Federico, Cipe Pineles, Paul Rand, and others in the 1940s and 1950s.

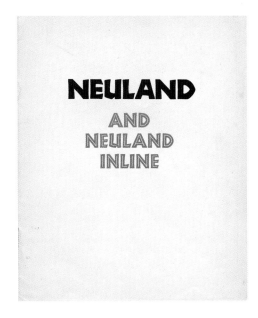

Neuland and Neuland Inline
Typefaces, 1923
Designer: Rudolf Koch (1876-1934)
Publisher: Gebr. Klingspor, Offenbach, and The Continental Typefounders, New York

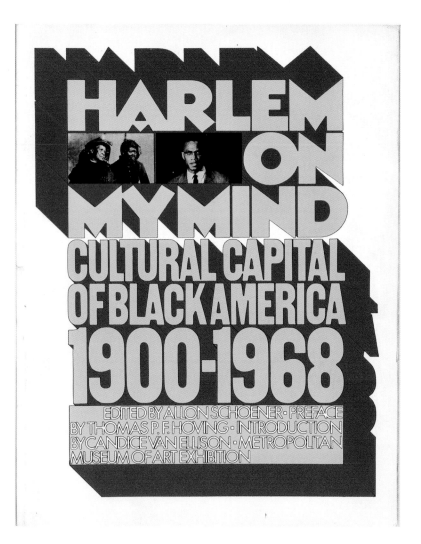

AA ABC C A C D E
FFA G G A H I J K K A
L LA LA M M N N T O P

Avant Garde
Design for typeface, 1967,
ink and gouache
Designer: Tom Carnase (b. 1939)
Firm: Lubalin, Smith, and Carnase Inc.
Collection Cooper-Hewitt, National
Design Museum, Gift of the designer

AMERICA is Boys To

AMERICA is the wool of Wa

AMERICA IS THE AROMA OF EVERGE

AMERICA is faithful Old Fait

AMERICA is Meatballs at Alice's Resta

AMERICA is grits and g

AMERICA IS THE PROWESS OF SKYSCRA

Harlem on My Mind
Book cover, 1968, offset lithograph
Designers: Herb Lubalin (1918-1981)
and Ernie Smith
Art director: Harris Lewine
Publisher: Random House, New York

Americana Alphabets
Catalog of typefaces, 1967,
offset lithograph
Designer: Ed Benguiat (b. 1927)
Publisher: Photo-Lettering, Inc., New York
Collection Cooper-Hewitt, National
Design Museum, Gift of Howard Goldstein

ERICA is rush hour on the BMT

ERICA is Reno's one-armed bandits

ERICA is Gullibles for Gutenberg's Galaxy

AERICA IS STARS & STRIPES

MERICA IS BIGTHINK

MERICA IS VALLEY FORGE

AMERICA is NOW!

The work of Herb Lubalin epitomized the eclectic transformation of the familiar in American commercial typography in the 1960s and 1970s. Lubalin exploited the potentials of phototypesetting by employing tight letter spacing and densely overlapping forms, gestures prohibited by the older metal technology. Lubalin abandoned standards of legibility and classical proportions in favor of exaggerating the distinctive features of letterforms—rounder *o*'s, sharper serifs, clever ligatures, and thin strokes reduced to minimal slivers. Working with designer and lettering artist Tom Carnase in New York, Lubalin created voluptuous interpretations of Victorian ornament and Pop revisions of modernist geometry.

Their typeface Avant Garde (1967), which drew inspiration from such modernist masterpieces as Paul Renner's Futura (1928), incorporates numerous composite characters and letters drawn with contorted angles. Designed by Carnase and inspired by Lubalin's logo for *Avant Garde* magazine, the typeface rejected modernism's search for reduction and efficiency in favor of a profusion of humorously idiosyncratic forms. The typefaces designed by Lubalin's contemporary Ed Benguiat also celebrated eclecticism and ornament, exploiting phototypesetting's capacity to reproduce illustrative, decorative forms.

Calling his approach "typographic expressionism," Lubalin defined his work as part of a uniquely American response to European modernism.[12] Looking back in 1979 at the achievements of his generation, Lubalin contrasted the "conglomerate styles" that were typical of American design

39

12. Lubalin called himself a "typographic expressionist" in his essay "The Graphic Revolution in America: Forty Years of Innovative Typography, 1940-1980," *Print* 33, 3 (May 1979): 41-85. See also Gertrude Snyder and Alan Peckolick, *Herb Lubalin: Art Director, Graphic Designer, and Typographer* (New York: American Showcase, 1985).

Tomato: Something Unusual is Going On Here
Poster, 1978, offset lithograph
Designer: Milton Glaser (b. 1929)
Publisher: The Tomato Music Company, New York
Collection Cooper-Hewitt, National Design Museum

One Line Manual of Photolettering Alphabets
Type catalog, 1988 (first issued 1960), offset lithograph
Designer unknown
Publisher: Photo-Lettering, Inc., New York

with the purism and abstraction favored in Europe—especially
Switzerland—after World War II:

> Typographic expressionism is for a mass audience. The more
> intellectual Bauhaus style and the formalized Swiss approach to
> design had no appeal and did not relate to the rank-and-file
> American. This work had its validity in the business community
> and in such special interest groups as the medical profession,
> and it still does. Americans...possess the most colorful language
> in the world, borrowing expressions and incorporating words
> primarily from the Jewish and Black vernacular....Precise
> intellectual design is not our bag: ideation is.

Popular rather than scholarly, Lubalin's approach was widely
imitated, shaping the mainstream of graphic design during
the span of his career.

The Push Pin Studio, founded in 1954, also reveled in the
mixing of historical and vernacular idioms. Based in New York,
the studio became an international force in graphic design in
the 1960s and 1970s; the group's impact remains profound
today. Milton Glaser and Seymour Chwast, the studio's most
celebrated founding members, are skilled typographers as
well as illustrators and designers. The "Push Pin style" has
yielded images that are personal yet highly controlled,
characterized by bright colors, strong outlines, and plump,
exaggerated forms.[13]

Herb Lubalin and the Push Pin artists opened up a path
in American design that has continued to evolve. The album
covers that Paula Scher designed for CBS Records in the late

Peugeot
Poster, c. 1968, offset lithograph
Designer: Seymour Chwast (b. 1931)
Art director: Robert Delpire
Publisher: Peugeot, Paris
Collection Cooper-Hewitt, National
Design Museum

Japanese Melodies for Flute and Harp
Album cover, front and back, 1978,
offset lithograph
Designer: Paula Scher (b. 1948)
Publisher: Columbia Records, New York
Collection Cooper-Hewitt, National
Design Museum, Gift of the designer

13. *The Push Pin Style* (Palo Alto,
California: Communication Arts
Magazine, 1970); Seymour Chwast,
The Left-Handed Designer (New York:
Harry N. Abrams, 1985); and Milton
Glaser, *Graphic Design* (Woodstock,
New York: Overlook Press, 1973).

COCA Season Poster (The Night Gallery)
Poster, 1991, offset lithograph
Designer: Art Chantry (b. 1954)
Publisher: Center on Contemporary Art, Seattle
Collection Cooper-Hewitt, National Design
Museum, Gift of the designer

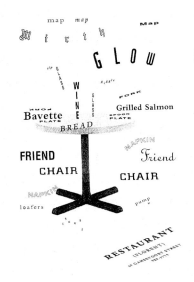

1970s tapped the history of design—from Art Nouveau to Russian Constructivism—for styles suited to the popular medium of music packaging. Scher founded the design studio Koppel and Scher in 1984 and joined the New York partnership Pentagram in 1991. Scher's loose interpretations of history ignore the philosophical ambitions behind aesthetic movements in favor of mining their emotional impact. In Scher's words, "I would rather be the Beatles than Philip Glass."[14] Neither nostalgic nor academic, Scher's work treats history as a warehouse of mannerisms and motifs to be used for their immediate appeal to contemporary audiences. Other designers working in this eclectic vein include Charles S. Anderson in Minneapolis, Art Chantry in Seattle, John Sayles in Des Moines, and Woody Pirtle in Dallas and New York.

Another approach to typographic eclecticism is seen in the studio M&Co., open in New York from 1979 to 1993. Under the direction of Tibor Kalman, M&Co. embraced the ready-made aesthetic of dictionaries, instruction manuals, and generic highway signs. Kalman viewed these unpretentious objects of daily life—produced outside the design profession—as examples of direct communication that could be appropriated for more sophisticated uses and injected into the context of contemporary design with a sense of irony. M&Co. turned the matter-of-fact vernacular of commercial printing into a clever, word-based approach to typography.[15]

Many younger designers, including Alexander Isley, Bethany Johns, Marlene McCarty, and Emily Oberman, passed through the M&Co. office during the 1980s, where they created concrete visual forms to embody Kalman's polemics.

Lunch, Brunch, Supper
Postcard, c. 1985, offset lithograph
Designers: Tibor Kalman (b. 1949) and
Alexander Isley (b. 1961)
Firm: M&Co.
Photographer: Neil Seilkirk
Publisher: Restaurant Florent, New York
Collection Cooper-Hewitt, National
Design Museum, Gift of Tibor Kalman

Restaurant Florent
Postcard, c. 1987, offset lithograph
Designer: Marlene McCarty (b. 1957)
Art director: Tibor Kalman
Firm: M&Co.
Publisher: Restaurant Florent, New York
Collection Cooper-Hewitt, National
Design Museum, Gift of Tibor Kalman

43

14. Paula Scher, interview with author, New York, August 1995. See also Philip B. Meggs, "The Women Who Saved New York!" *Print* 43, 1 (January/February 1989): 61-71.

15. M&Co. received signficant coverage in the general press. See Patricia Leigh Brown, "Graphic Design Out of a Utopian Past," *New York Times*, February 11, 1988.

BORROMINI PIRANDELLO BARBERINI VIGNELLI
MORAVIA BOCCIONI COLOMBO PUCCINI RADICE
CROCE DECARLO PERUZZI CIMABUE PALLADIO
AULENTI GALILEO BRAMANTE BALLA ARMANI
RAGGI MENOTTI FELLINI MENDINI PININFARINA
PAGANINI GIORGIONE NOORDA BERNINI VASARI
CARAVAGGIO BURRI PIRANESI PIERO GIUGIARO
MADERNO NERVI NERONE PASOLINI DONIZETTI
ROSSI TOSCANINI LEOPARDI AGNELLI FERRARI
ORSINI VERDI DONATELLO CENCI SAVONAROLA
FIORUCCI ZEFFIRELLI LIPPI GREGOTTI GUCCI
MAZZEI BRION CERATTO VOLTA SPQR ZANUSO
STRADIVARI GIURGOLA VALENTINO PETRARCA
BRUNELLESCHI BOTTICELLI SCOLA BOCCACCIO
MODIGLIANI CARUSO MANGIONE DEBENEDETTI
GRUCCI CASTAGNOLI PIANO LEONARDO CELLINI
SOTTSASS BERTOLUCCI FERMI CHIGI CASANOVA
BORGIA MARINETTI VALLE ANTONIONI MEDICI
MASACCIO ZEVI ALBERTI WOJTYLA CICERONE
CESARE GARIBALDI BELLINI RESPIGHI MAZZINI
SARTOGO VESPUCCI BENE FALLACI BORGHESE
MACHIAVELLI BARZINI CANOVA SOAVI NICOLAO
FARNESE GIOTTO LOLLOBRIGIDA ECO ROSSINI
CASSINA MARCONI TIZIANO MISSONI ARBASINO
TINTORETTO VILLAGIO VIVALDI QUILICI PESCE
BUGATTI LIONNI BILLESI PECCEI MONTESSORI
RAFFAELLO BODONI OLIVETTI MICHELANGELO
DANTE ETCETERA ETCETERA THE ITALIAN IDEA

INTERNATIONAL DESIGN CONFERENCE IN ASPEN 1981   JUNE 14 TO 19

The Italian Idea
Poster, 1981, offset lithograph
Designer: George Sadek (b. 1928) and Tom Kluepfel
Firm: Center for Design and Typography, The Cooper Union
Publisher: International Design Conference in Aspen
Collection Cooper-Hewitt, National Design Museum

Several important studios were directly influenced by M&Co., including Drenttel Doyle Partners, founded in 1985 by William Drenttel, Stephen Doyle, and Tom Kluepfel. Designers Doyle and Kluepfel, former employees of M&Co., have implemented structures from the history of printing in new scales and contexts. In their work, the classical book collides with the modern magazine. Typographic conventions such as initial caps, footnotes, side bars, and borders become poster-sized elements bursting off the page or minute details packed into the margins.[16]

The fascination with language seen at M&Co. and many of the studios that formed in its wake reflects the influence of The Cooper Union in New York, which was a maelstrom of competing design ideologies in the 1970s and 1980s. The school is the alma mater of Milton Glaser, Seymour Chwast, Herb Lubalin, and Lou Dorfsman, giants of the design world who influenced the school as members of the adjunct faculty and the board of trustees. Another powerful force was Rudolph de Harak, a teacher and designer whose rational, systems-based design methodology contrasted with the eclectic populism practiced by Glaser and others.

Between these opposing forces stood a unique figure: George Sadek, a Czech emigré who mixed the traditions of concrete poetry, classical typography, and the European avant-garde. Sadek is neither a free-wheeling eclectic nor a doctrinaire rationalist; his design courses stressed verbal play over stylistic appropriation, approaching typography as a literary and conceptual medium. Many of Sadek's students carried his subtly deranged classicism—what Tom Kluepfel

44

16. William Drenttel and Stephen Doyle, interview with author, New York, July 1994. See also Steven Heller, "Champions of the New Classicism," *I.D.* (January/February 1994): 44.

17. See the exhibition catalog, *George Sadek and Friends* (New York: The Cooper Union, 1993).

has called "lunacy over logic"—into their professional work, including Kluepfel, Stephen Doyle, Alexander Isley, J. Abbott Miller, Mike Mills, Charles Nix, and Emily Oberman. Sadek retired from The Cooper Union in 1993.[17]

From typefaces drawn from classical and vernacular sources to books and posters that play with historical styles and structures, an important track of innovation in contemporary design openly engages an existing culture of signs, symbols, and styles. Such work builds upon a taut yet permeable web of visual literacy, a common language in which elements move in and out of currency, their meaning open to continual revision. The best work transforms the meaning of the old and the ordinary while drawing energy from its tremendous power to communicate.

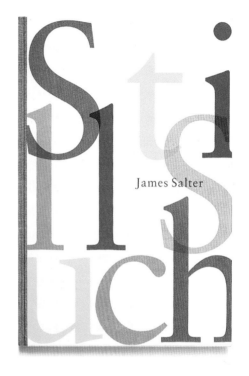

Still Such
Book, 1992, offset lithograph
Designer: Stephen Doyle (b. 1956)
Publisher: William Drenttel, New York
Collection Cooper-Hewitt, National
Design Museum, Gift of William Drenttel

she wore at the reception and then more firsts, apartment near Gracie Square, clever dog, first real money a fifteen thousand dollar check, first child a girl, Sunday mornings, winter city silver and grey, silent windows along Madison, colors of Sonia Delaunay, rich friends in the sixties dressing for the evening, cufflinks dense gold, wives deep in sofas,

Stadttheater Basel
Poster, 1960, offset lithograph
Designer: Armin Hofmann (b. 1920)
Publisher: Stadttheater Basel
Collection Cooper-Hewitt, National Design
Museum, Gift of the Estate of Dan Friedman

REINVENTING
THE
MODERN

While some contemporary designers have sought to expand the history of their medium by revising historical forms and structures, another stream in current practice is directed toward developing a vision of the future. Many innovations in design over the past two decades derive from an active and skeptical exploration of the avant-garde movements that revolutionized art and design in the early twentieth century.

In the 1920s, members of the avant-garde sought to replace past styles with new forms that reflected the emerging mechanics of motion pictures and the mass media. Many designers today embrace the modernist ambition to create an experimental visual language that hinges on technology and turns against the past. These same designers, however, have rejected the ideal of a purified, objective, and universal mode of communication articulated by avant-garde designers and typographers in the 20s. In its place, they have promoted personal expression and a vocabulary that mixes modernist geometries with references to popular culture.

Constructivist designers working in the Soviet Union, Germany, the Netherlands, and other parts of Europe between the World Wars dissected the technologies of the graphic arts—photography, typography, photomechanical reproduction—in order to synthesize a new language of vision

46

Helvetica

appropriate to the rapid pace of industrial life. In the 1930s many avant-garde artists emigrated to the United States, where they sought to assimilate modernist forms and theories into the world's most developed consumer culture. A generation of Americans, led by Lester Beall, Paul Rand and Bradbury Thompson, worked alongside European expatriates including Herbert Bayer, Alexey Brodovitch, and Will Burtin. This commercial vanguard transformed American printed media by fitting modernist aesthetics to the interests of corporate communications and popular publishing.[18]

A second wave of European modernism arrived in the United States via Switzerland in the late 1950s, when schools of design in Basel and Zurich were refining the experiments of the avant-garde into a rational, systematic methodology. Armin Hofmann, Josef Müller-Brockmann, Emil Ruder, and others validated sans serif typefaces, stark photographs, geometric symbols, and gridded page layouts as the basis of a universal language, whose abstract forms would communicate ideas directly to the eye.[19] A small subculture of the American design profession embraced this methodology in the 1960s and 1970s. The typeface Helvetica—whose name is derived from *Helvetia*, meaning Switzerland—became synonymous with so-called "Swiss design."

Massimo Vignelli has been a passionate protagonist of rational design theory in the United States. Born in Italy in 1931 and trained as an architect, Vignelli worked with the Swiss graphic designer Max Huber during the 1950s and emigrated to the United States in 1965. Known for his use of strong horizontal "information bands" and for his unwavering

Skyline
Magazine, 1978, offset lithograph
Designer: Massimo Vignelli (b. 1931)
Design assistant: Lorraine Wild (b. 1953)
Publisher: Institute for Architecture and Urban Studies, New York

47

18. Lorraine Wild, "Europeans in America," in *Graphic Design in America: A Visual Language History*, ed. Mildred Friedman (Minneapolis: Walker Art Center, 1989), 153-169.

19. Philip B. Meggs, "The Swiss Influence: The Old New Wave," *AIGA Journal of Graphic Design* 4, 1 (1986).

Kreative Tief Phase
Poster, 1972, offset lithograph
Designer: Wolfgang Weingart (b. 1941)
Collection Cooper-Hewitt,
National Design Museum,
Gift of the Estate of Dan Friedman

commitment to a narrow canon of elegant, legible typefaces, Vignelli has consistently promoted rational modernism as a typographic method with universal validity.[20]

At the same time as this rational typographic approach was emerging as a minority voice within the American design profession, it was already under attack back home in Switzerland. In the late 1960s, Wolfgang Weingart, teaching at Basel's Kunstgewerbeschule (School of Design), began to build complex, overtly personal page compositions out of modernism's vocabulary of grids, bars, open spaces, and unadorned letterforms. Recalling the "new typography" theorized by Jan Tschichold in the 1920s, Weingart's revision of avant-garde principles became known as the "new typography" in the 1970s and 1980s. He initiated a reactive phase of modernism that has profoundly shaped graphic design in the United States.[21]

The American designer Dan Friedman went to study at the Kunstgewerbeschule in 1968, the same year Weingart began teaching there. After returning to the United States to teach at the Yale School of Art and the State University of New York, in Purchase, Friedman sought to ground Weingart's "new typography" in an explicit methodology. A pedagogical manifesto he published in the journal *Visible Language* in 1973 influenced design courses across the United States. The essay, which features typographic interpretations of a weather report, rejects the objective standard of "legibility" and replaces it with the overtly relativized theory of "readability." Friedman argued that complex arrangements can engage an audience's intelligence and emotions.

48

20. "Massimo Vignelli vs. Ed Benguiat," interview with Philip Meggs, *Print* 45, 8 (September/ October 1991): 88-95.
21. *Design Quarterly* 130 (1985) juxtaposes essays by Armin Hofmann and Wolfgang Weingart.
22. Dan Friedman, interview with author, New York, June 1994. See also Dan Friedman, *Radical Modernism* (Yale University Press, 1994); and "A View: Introductory Education in Typography," *Visible Language* 7, 2 (spring 1973): 129-144.
23. April Greiman, *Hybrid Imagery* (New York: Watson-Guptill, 1990).

Through his teaching as well as his practice as a corporate designer in the 1970s, Friedman became a leading spokesman for the new typography. In 1994, he recalled:

> Unlike Wolfgang Weingart, I wasn't reacting *against* Swiss typography, because that rational system didn't really exist in the United States except in isolated instances. Whereas Weingart was teaching based on intuition, I was trying to verbalize and demystify the structures of typography. I wanted to create a method. I had to find a way to teach the rules and also how to break them at the same time, since nobody knew the rules.[22]

Friedman recognized the tenuous position of modernist graphic design in America: because rationalist methods had never been firmly established here, both the new typography and the rational system that it rejected carried a progressive edge. For young American designers, the new typography did not simply revise a stale and discredited tradition, but brought with it knowledge of the radical formalism of the European avant-garde. Friedman showed young designers how to honor and challenge the principles of modernism simultaneously.

Weingart's American students included April Greiman, who, returning to work in Los Angeles in 1976, infused the new typography with energetic impulses from punk culture. Her 1979 logo for the boutique Vertigo mixes styles, weights, and sizes of letterforms and floats them in an ambiguous frame against various patterns. Greiman's work in the 1980s and 1990s embraced digital technology both as a means of production and source of mystical inspiration; she developed an image of the designer as technological visionary.[23]

Hot and Sunny
Pedagogical exercise, 1973
Designer: Dan Friedman (1946–1995)
Publisher: *Visible Language,* Cleveland

Vertigo
Business cards, 1979, offset lithograph
Designer: April Greiman (b. 1948)
Publisher: Vertigo, Los Angeles
Collection Cooper-Hewitt, National Design
Museum, Gift of the designer

49

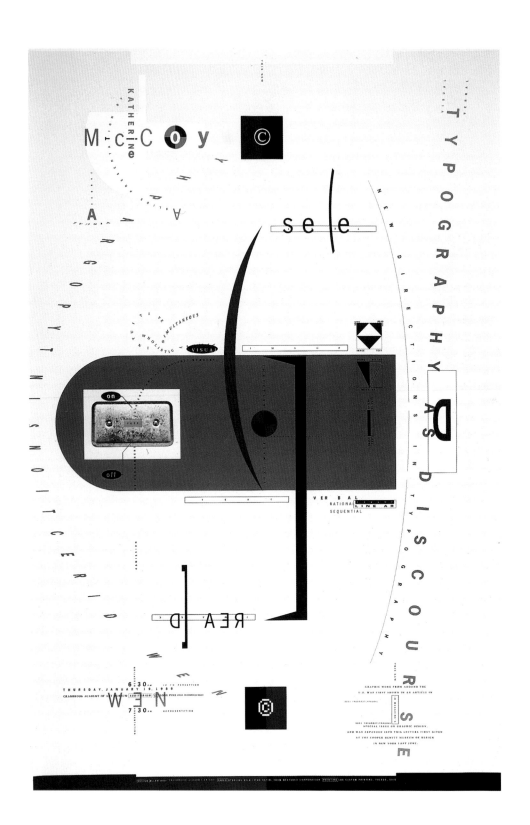

Typography as Discourse
Poster, 1989, offset lithograph
Designer: Allen Hori (b. 1960)
Publisher: Cranbrook Academy of Art,
Bloomfield Hills, Michigan
Collection Cooper-Hewitt, National
Design Museum, Gift of Katherine McCoy

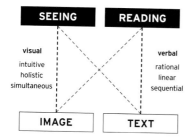

Typography as Discourse
Diagram, 1990
Designer/author: Katherine McCoy
Publisher: *Design Quarterly,*
Minneapolis

Typography as Discourse
Poster, 1991, offset lithograph
Designers: Andrew Blauvelt (b. 1964),
James Sholly (b. 1965), and
Laura Lacy-Sholly (b. 1965)
Publisher: Art Director's Club of
Indiana, Indianaoplis
Collection Cooper-Hewitt,
National Design Museum,
Gift of Andrew Blauvelt

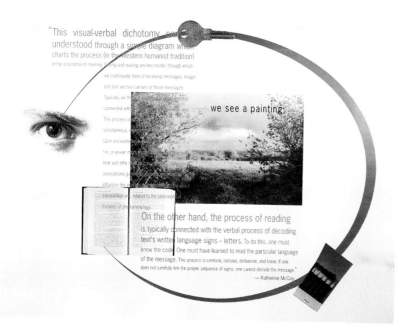

Whereas Herb Lubalin's typographic expressionism and its offshoots constituted a kind of commercial populism, Weingart's new typography developed as an intellectual discourse allied with high culture and critical self-consciousness. Associated with teaching from its inception, the new typography molded the thought of a generation of American educators, from Philadelphia to Los Angeles.

The new typography flourished at the Cranbrook Academy of Art in Bloomfield Hills, Michigan, which became a center for experimental design in the 1970s and 1980s. The design program there was jointly headed by graphic designer Katherine McCoy and product designer Michael McCoy from 1971 through 1995. Although the McCoys began their work at Cranbrook as committed modernists, by the mid-1970s they had joined the rebellion against rational problem-solving in favor of expressive formalism.[24] In the 1980s Katherine McCoy and her students developed a model of "typography as discourse." They argued that by layering and juxtaposing words and pictures, designers construct compositions that demand to be interpreted on their own terms, beyond their objective content. Influenced by post-structuralist literary theory, McCoy rejected the traditional distinction between reading and seeing, arguing that designers should actively mix these categories of experience: a picture can be read, while written words can be objects of vision.

51

24. Katherine McCoy, "American Graphic Design Expression," *Design Quarterly* 148 (1990): 4-22. See also Hugh Aldersey-Williams et al., *Cranbrook: The New Design Discourse* (New York: Rizzoli, 1990); and Ellen Lupton, "The Academy of Deconstructed Design," *Eye* 1, 3 (winter 1991): 44-52.

De Nieuwe: An Exhibition of Recent
Graphic Design from the Netherlands
Poster, 1987, offset lithograph
Designer: Lucille Tenazas (b. 1953)
Publisher: American Institute of Graphic Arts,
San Francisco Chapter
Collection Cooper-Hewitt, National
Design Museum, Gift of the designer

Weingart, a frequent lecturer at Cranbrook during the 1970s and 1980s, helped infuse the program with the expressionism of the new typography. To Weingart's minimalist language the McCoys added ideas from the architectural theory of Robert Venturi and Denise Scott Brown. These architects had legitimized the "commercial vernacular" of suburban shopping districts as an indigenous expression of American culture. McCoy encouraged her students to mix the austere vocabulary of modernism with elements from mainstream media.

Around 1984 the Dutch designer Gert Dumbar brought another revision of European modernism to Cranbrook. Studio Dumbar complicated the Swiss vocabulary with references to classical typography and Baroque painting, using dramatically staged still-life photographs as a ground for finely wrought typographic compositions. Trips to the Netherlands by young American designers began replacing journeys to Switzerland, while Dumbar and other Dutch designers lectured across the United States.[25]

While the new typography of the 1970s conducted its formal experiments with a canon of such modernist typefaces as Futura, Helvetica, and Univers, the digital revolution spurred the production of countless new fonts.[26] Emigre Fonts was founded in 1984 by Rudy Vanderlans and Zuzana Licko in Oakland, California. Digital typefaces designed by Licko and others were featured in *Emigre*, a magazine edited and art directed by Vanderlans. *Emigre* quickly became an international fan magazine devoted to experimental design and typography.[27]

Zee Belt
Logo, c. 1989
Designer: Vincent van Baar,
Firm: Studio Dumbar
Client: Zee Belt Theater, The Hague

Fact Twenty Two
Poster, 1990, offset lithograph
Designer: Rudy Vanderlans (b. 1955)
Photographer: James Towning
Publisher: Emigre, Sacramento
Collection Cooper-Hewitt, National
Design Museum, Gift of the designer

53

25. See Ellen Lupton, "American Dutch/Dutch American: Hands Across the Zee," *Print* 45, 6 (November/December 1991): 116-125.
26. On type design in the early 1990s, see Jonathan Barnbrook, "Fonts Set Free," *Design* 514 (October 1991): 24-7.

27. Rudy Vanderlans, Zuzana Licko, and Mary E. Grey, *Emigre: Graphic Design into the Digital Realm* (New York: Van Nostrand Reinhold, 1994). See also Zuzana Licko and Rudy Vanderlans, "The New Primitives," *I.D.* 35, 2 (March/April 1988): 60.

Variex, typeface, 1988
Designers: Zuzana Licko (b. 1961)
and Rudy Vanderlans (b. 1955)
Courtesy Emigre Fonts, Sacramento

... which evolved from the process of adjusting the positive and negative space as necessary to balance the element visually within the structure of a particular repetition sequence.

Soda Script Light

AaBbCcDdEe
FfGgHhIi
IjK kL Mm
NnOoP pQ
qR r
Ss TtUuV Ww
XxYy Zz

Soda Script Bold

AaBbCcDdEeF
fGgH
hIi IjK kL I
Mm NnOoP
pQ qR r
Ss TtUuVv
WwXxYy Zz

Journal AaBbCcDdEeFfGgHhIiJjKkLl

Elektrix (1989), *Whirligigs*
(1994), *Soda Script* (1995), and
Journal (1990)
Typefaces
Designer: Zuzana Licko
Courtesy Emigre Fonts,
Sacramento

Emigre Fonts successfully marketed typefaces for use on microcomputers and became a model for other independent font producers. Companies that market experimental digital typefaces include GarageFonts in Del Mar, California, [T26] and Thirstype in Chicago, House Industries in Wilmington, The American Type Corporation in Indianapolis, and the international company FontShop, all founded in the early to mid-1990s. The dissemination of typefaces has become a form of underground publishing, in which the medium is, quite literally, the message.

Licko's typefaces often recall the 1920s fascination with geometrically constructed letterforms. At the Bauhaus, Herbert Bayer and Josef Albers had assembled letterforms out of restricted repertoires of geometric shapes; the design of these visionary alphabets emulated the methods of mass production. Many of Licko's first typefaces were designed to accommodate the coarse, low-resolution forms and reduced range of curves and angles permitted by early laser printers and video display terminals. Licko built the Variex family of typefaces (1988) around a simple geometric armature that systematically expands to produce bolder weights.

Licko's typeface Journal (1990) turned toward a more narrative sensibility. The abrupt contours of Journal loosely suggest the battered forms of typewriter manuscripts and newsprint pages as well as the geometric outlines favored by digital printing. Whirligigs (1994) uses the principle of modular construction to generate dense ornamental patterns, while Soda (1995) is a set of script letterforms that couple with lyrical swashes.

Urban Font Culture
Sticker, 1994, offset lithograph
Designer unknown
New York City

GarageFonts
Type catalog, 1994, offset lithograph
Designers: Brian Kelly (b. 1967)
and Nancy Mazzei (b. 1967)
Courtesy GarageFonts, Del Mar,
California

55

Lovenote/Hatenote and *Stroke*
Typefaces, 1995
Designers: Chester (Lovenote) and
Frank Ford (Stroke) (b. 1951)
Specimen designed by Rick Valicenti
Courtesy Thirstype, Barrington, Illinois

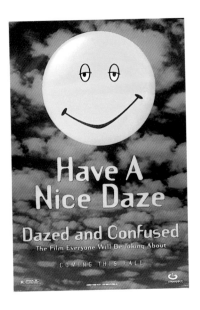

Template Gothic GgHhIiJjKkLlMmNnOoPpQqRr

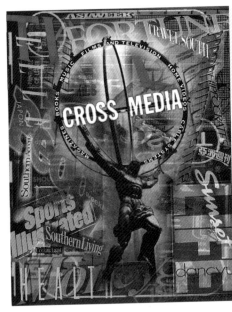

Lift and Separate
Postcard, 1993, offset lithograph
Designer: Barbara Glauber (b. 1962)
Publisher: The Cooper Union, New York
Collection Cooper-Hewitt, National
Design Museum, Gift of the designer

Template Gothic
Typeface, 1990
Designer: Barry Deck (b. 1962)
Courtesy Emigre Fonts, Sacramento

Dazed and Confused
Poster, 1994, offset lithograph
Designer unknown

Time Warner 1990 Annual Report
Annual report, 1991, offset lithograph
Designers: Kent Hunter (b. 1956)
and Ruth Deiner (b. 1966)
Creative directors: Aubrey Balkind
(b. 1944) and Kent Hunter
Firm: Frankfurt Gips Balkind
Publisher: Time Warner, Inc., New York

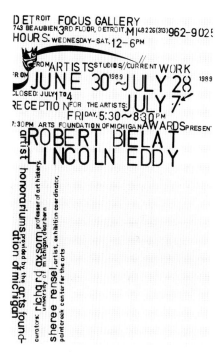

Dramatic experiments with narrative typography have been performed by Edward Fella, who attended Cranbrook following a two-decade career as a self-taught graphic designer. Since graduating from Cranbrook in 1987 at age forty-eight, Fella has taught at the California Institute of the Arts (CalArts). In his work, damaged and defective forms—from third-generation photocopies to broken pieces of transfer type—are assembled by means of Fella's formidable yet technologically out-of-date manual skills, including hand lettering and meticulous paste-up production. In Fella's work, the unfettered mind of a Dada/Fluxus hippie confronts the dexterous hand of a traditional commercial artist. Fella designed over sixty posters for the Detroit Focus Gallery between 1987 and 1990. The gallery, by giving Fella total freedom in designing these low-budget posters, provided a public outlet for experimental design.[28]

Fella has rarely worked with computers, relying instead on a battery of hand skills that have become nearly obsolete. Yet his work has a structural affinity with digitally produced typography. In Fella's words,

> I actually feel that I started thinking like a computer a while back, almost inadvertently or instinctively. Some of my work preceded the computer, in that I was doing all these things that were difficult to do manually, but are so obvious and easy to do on the computer, like the mixes of typefaces, the slight differences in size, the distortions, the irregularities....I just avoided the first phase of the computer, the bitmap phase.[29]

While Fella has sidestepped the computer, his students—including Barry Deck, who began designing typefaces while

Robert Bielat/Lincoln Eddy
Poster, 1989, offset lithograph
Designer: Edward Fella (b. 1938)
Publisher: Detroit Focus Gallery
Collection Cooper-Hewitt, National
Design Museum, Gift of the designer

Sculpture
Poster, 1990, offset lithograph
Designer: Edward Fella
Publisher: Detroit Focus Gallery
Collection Cooper-Hewitt, National
Design Museum, Gift of the designer

28. See Rick Poynor, "Out There: Ed Fella," *Frieze* (summer 1992): 49-51.
29. Quote from "A Conversation, Edward Fella and Mr. Keedy," *Emigre* 17 (1991): 13-15.

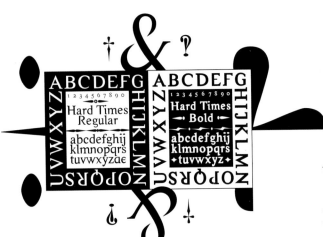

attending Cal Arts—are avid users. Deck's Template Gothic, which debuted in the pages of *Emigre* in 1990, was a response to one of Fella's handmade posters. Generated in the digital environment, the bruised characters of Template Gothic are soft and organic yet linked to the industrial realm of mass-produced stencils.[30]

Another creator of narrative typography is Jeffery Keedy, who received his MFA from Cranbrook in 1985 and now teaches at Cal Arts. His typeface Hard Times (1991) revises and reassembles the elements of a modern classic— Times Roman. Manusans (1990) quotes elementary school penmanship. Although several of Keedy's own typefaces are based on historical sources, his fonts are ironic commentaries, not scholarly revivals. Keedy has argued that designers should search for the future rather than excavate the past. In his model of an ever-improving design language, new typefaces are fuel for engines of perpetual progress.[31]

Pronouncing that "You can't do new typography with old typefaces," Keedy has countered the modernist principle that graphic design is an art of manipulating an exisiting lexicon of visual material.[32] El Lissitzky, John Heartfield, and other avant-gardists of the 1920s used cameras, scissors, glue, and the ready-made equipment of the commercial print shop to record and reorganize cultural signs. For the Constructivist *photomonteur*, "newness" resulted from surprising uses of the everyday, defamiliarized through technological means.

What constitutes the "new" is an uncertain question in contemporary culture. How quickly does a typeface get old? Zuzana Licko's Matrix, for example, was born into a vanguard

Hard Times
Typeface, 1991
Designer:
Jeffery Keedy (b. 1957)
Courtesy FontShop
International

Keedy Sans
Typeface, 1989
Designer:
Jeffery Keedy
Courtesy Emigre Fonts,
Sacramento

Manusans
Typeface, 1990
Designer:
Jeffery Keedy
Courtesy FontShop
International

30. On Template Gothic, see Rick Poynor, "American Gothic," *Eye* 2, 6 (autumn 1992): 64-67; and Michael Bierut, "American Gothic: Barry Deck and Barry Deck Design," *I.D.* (January/February 1994): 43. Template Gothic debuted in *Emigre* 15 (1990).

31. Jeffery Keedy, interview, *Emigre* 15 (1990): 14-17. On different ways designers approach the historical revival of typefaces, see John Downer, "Copping an Attitude, Part 2," *Emigre* 38 (1996): 10-19.

Matrix

subculture in 1986, and has since appeared in a Cadillac ad, a McDonald's placemat, and other unlikely places for the avant-garde to take root. Barry Deck's Template Gothic, initiated as a student experiment, has found its way onto annual reports and network television. In a high-speed playback of history, these fonts are very old indeed.

Post-modernism, a word Keedy freely employs in his own writing, proposes a problematic relationship to the "new." The term entered the popular mainstream in the 1970s and 1980s, referring to techniques of pastiche and appropriation, from the neo-classical nostalgia of Philip Johnson's AT&T tower in New York to the overtly artificial identities of Madonna and Cindy Sherman. Post-modernism identifies a position *after* originality, beyond the period of belief in the continual remaking of civilization. As cultural critic Hal Foster has argued, post-modernism is not just an artistic style but a condition of life in a media-saturated world, embracing everything from art and music to the network news.[33]

As a new typeface enters the currency of cultural use, it becomes part of history. The impurities of quotation can convert any unique gesture, endowed with the personality of its maker, into a sign, a repeatable mark. Some designers treat the past as a warehouse of images to be revised, repackaged, or transformed. Others try to escape from history, only to see it swallow up the fragile newness of their work. The mixing of styles and symbols is not only a deliberate strategy employed by individual artists; it is a symptom of the circulation of signs in contemporary culture.

Matrix
Typeface, 1986
Designer: Zuzana Licko (b. 1961)
Courtesy Emigre Fonts, Sacramento

Be Quake McSafe!
Tray liner, 1993, offset lithograph
Designers: Davis Ball & Colombatto Advertising
Publisher: McDonald's Operators Association of Southern California
Courtesy McDonald's Corporation

Cadillac DeVille
Advertisement, 1993, offset lithograph
Designer unknown
Courtesy Emigre Fonts, Sacramento

59

32. Jeffery Keedy, "The Rules of Typography According to Experts/ Crackpots," *Eye* 3, 11 (winter 1993): 48-55.
33. Hal Foster, "(Post)Modern Polemics," *Recodings* (Seattle: Bay Press, 1985): 121-137.

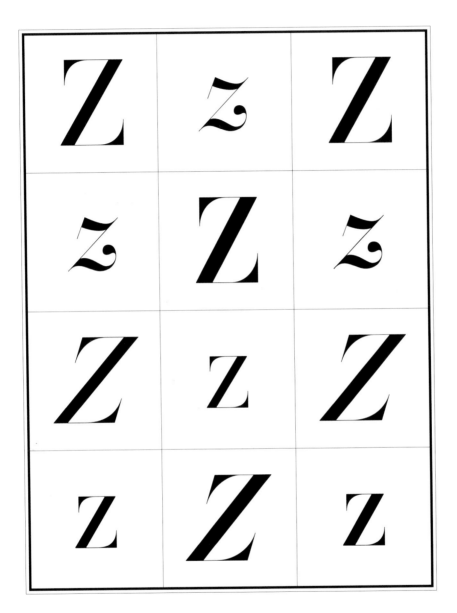

Didot
Typeface, 1992
Designer: Jonathan Hoefler (b. 1970)
Courtesy The Hoefler Type Foundry, New York

Jonathan Hoefler's revival of the eighteenth-
century typeface Didot was created for *Harper's
Bazaar,* redesigned by Fabien Baron in 1992.
By drawing special versions of the font for
reproduction at particular sizes, Hoefler insured
that the thin strokes of the characters remain
even when the letters are displayed at a large
scale. Bus Didot, for example, is used for
advertisements on the sides of buses.

Nobel Regular Nobel Bold

Armada Thin ArmadaThinCompressed

ArmadaBlack

GarageGothicRegularGarage GothicBoldGarageGothicBlack

Nobel
Typeface, originally designed by
Sjoerd Henrik de Roos, Amsterdam, 1929
Redesigned in 1993 by Tobias Frere-Jones (b. 1970)

Armada
Typeface, 1987–1994
Designer: Tobias Frere-Jones

Garage Gothic
Typeface, 1992
Designer: Tobias Frere-Jones

Courtesy Font Bureau, Boston

Tobias Frere-Jones's typeface designs for Font Bureau in Boston include historical revivals, such as Nobel, as well as faces that are based on loose historical references, such as Armada. According to Frere-Jones, Armada follows the "verticals and flat arches basic to the architectural geometry of nineteenth-century American cites." His typeface Garage Gothic was inspired by the numerals printed on parking-garage tickets.

BIG ED SR

BIG ED LAZYBOY

Hey Stupid Normal

Hey Stupid Duh

Hey Stupid Yup

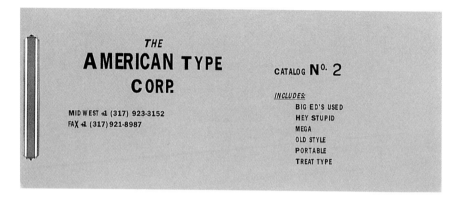

Big Ed and *Hey Stupid*
Typefaces, c. 1994
Designer: Edwin Utermohlen (b. 1954)
Courtesy The American Type Corp.,
Indianapolis

The American Type Corp.
Catalog, 1994, laser print
Designers: Jim Ross (b. 1966)
and Mario A. Mirelez (b. 1965)
Publisher: The American Type Corp.,
Indianapolis

Remedy
Typeface, 1991
Designer: Frank Heine
Courtesy Emigre Fonts, Sacramento

Dingura
Typeface, 1990
Designer: Carlos Segura (b. 1957)
Courtesy [T-26], Chicago

Roughhouse, typeface, 1992
Designer: Andy Cruz (b. 1972)

Crackhouse, typeface, 1994
Designer: Jeremy Dean (b. 1972)

Housemaid, typeface, 1994
Designer: Kristen Faulkner (b. 1970)

Courtesy House Industries, Wilmington

Roughhouse

Crackhouse

Housemaid

House Industries
Type catalog, 1994, offset lithograph
Art director and designer: Andy Cruz
Designers: Rich Roat (b. 1965) and
Allan Mercer (b. 1972)
Publisher: House Industries, Wilmington

Parkway, typeface family, 1994
Designer: Charles "Chank" Anderson (b. 1969)
Courtesy CAKEfonts, Minneapolis

Parkway Motel
Parkway MotorLodge
Parkway Resort-o-tel

With the rise of the desktop computer as the ubiquitous tool
of typographic design and production, many designers have
created fonts that reject slick, smooth geometries in favor
of damaged, irregular forms. Numerous small type businesses have opened since the early 1990s, making font
production a new form of underground publishing.

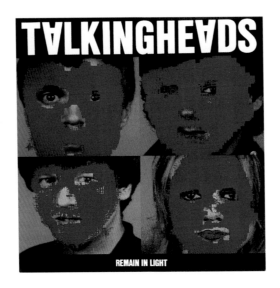

The New York studio M&Co. became notorious during the 1980s for work that rejected the values of corporate modernism in favor of a style that was deliberately blunt and direct. Games with language are central to many of M&Co.'s projects.

Talking Heads: Remain in Light
Album cover, front (above) and back (below),
1980, offset lithograph
Designers: Tibor Kalman (b. 1949) and Carol Bokuniewicz
Firm: M&Co.
Computer images: HCL, JPT, DDD, Walter GP, Paul, C/T
Publisher: Sire Records, New York
Collection Cooper-Hewitt, National
Design Museum, Gift of Tibor Kalman

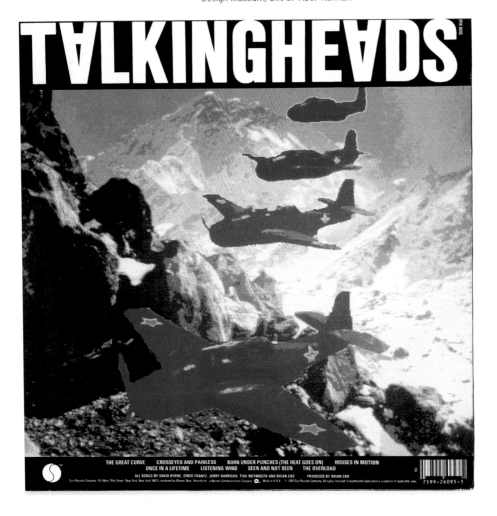

Jerry Harrison: Casual Gods
Album cover, 1988, offset lithograph
Designer: Emily Oberman (b. 1963)
Firm: M&Co.
Art director: Tibor Kalman
Publisher: Sire Records, New York
Collection Cooper-Hewitt, National
Design Museum, Gift of Tibor Kalman

DEFUNKT
Album cover, 1982, offset lithograph
Designer: Larry Kazal
Art director: Tibor Kalman
Firm: M&Co.
Publisher: Hannibal Records, Division
of Island Records, Inc., New York
Collection Cooper-Hewitt, National
Design Museum, Gift of Tibor Kalman

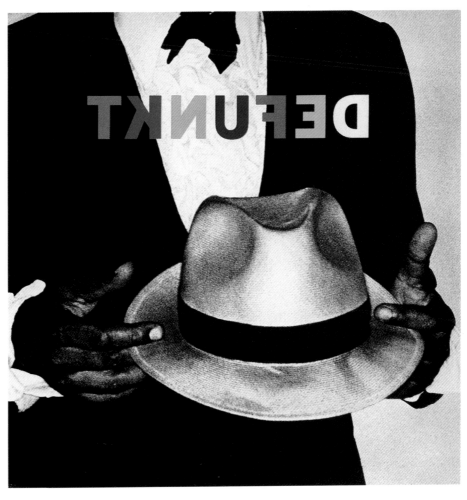

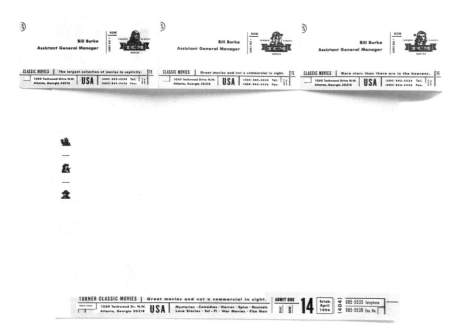

Turner Classic Movies
Stationery, 1994, offset lithograph
Designers: Charles S. Anderson (b. 1958),
Paul Howalt, and Joel Templin
Art director: Charles S. Anderson
Illustrators: Charles S. Anderson and Paul Howalt
Publisher: Turner Classic Movies, Atlanta
Collection Cooper-Hewitt, National Design
Museum, Gift of Charles S. Anderson

Charles S. Anderson is one of several designers
who has used the history of commercial printing
to revitalize design. Such vernacular artifacts as
movie tickets and printer's press proofs are the
basis of Anderson's tactile, decorative approach.

Four New Lines of Utility Paper
Poster printed in two pieces, 1994,
offset lithograph
Designer: Charles S. Anderson and
Todd Piper-Hauswirth (b. 1967)
Art director: Charles S. Anderson
Photographer: Paul Irmiter
Illustrations: CSA Archive Stock Image Collection
Publisher: French Paper Company, Niles, Michigan
Collection Cooper-Hewitt, National Design
Museum, Gift of Charles S. Anderson

801 Steak and Chop House
Shopping bag, 1993, offset lithograph
Designer: Sayles Graphic Design
Art director: John Sayles (b. 1958)
Publisher: 801 Steak and Chop House, Des Moines
Collection Cooper-Hewitt, National
Design Museum, Gift of John Sayles

Working in Des Moines, John Sayles often
grounds his work in regional references. This bag
for a steak house celebrates cattle as local color.

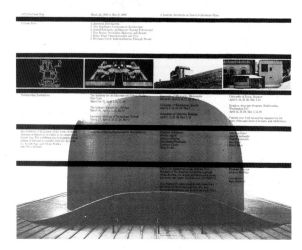

New Wave of Austrian Architecture
Poster, 1980, offset lithograph
Designer: Massimo Vignelli (b. 1931)
Publisher: Institute of Architecture
and Urban Studies, New York
Collection Cooper-Hewitt,
National Design Museum

Unfinished Modern
Poster, 1984, silkscreen
Designer: Michael Bierut (b. 1958)
Firm: Vignelli Associates
Publisher: The Architectural League
of New York, with Formica Corporation
Collection Cooper-Hewitt,
National Design Museum,
Gift of the designer

Monument Informal
Poster, 1985, silkscreen and crayon
Designer: Michael Bierut
Firm: Vignelli Associates
Publisher: The Architectural League
of New York, with Formica Corporation
Collection Cooper-Hewitt,
National Design Museum,
Gift of the designer

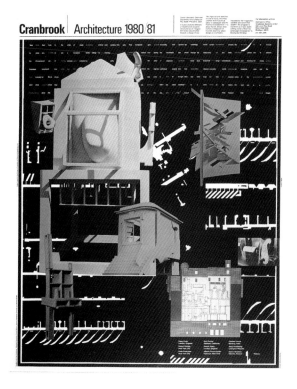

Cranbrook Architecture
Poster, 1980, offset lithograph
Designer: Katherine McCoy (b. 1945)
Publisher: Cranbrook Academy of Art,
Bloomfield Hills, Michigan
Collection Cooper-Hewitt, National Design
Museum, Gift of the designer

The Language of Michael Graves
Poster, 1983, offset lithograph
Designer: William Longhauser (b. 1947)
Publisher: Moore College of Art and
Design, Philadelphia
Collection Cooper-Hewitt, National Design
Museum, Gift of the designer

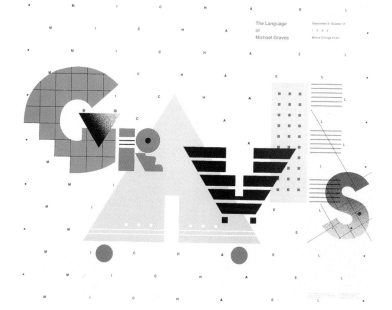

Post-modernism in architecture had entered the popular discourse by the beginning of the 1980s. In the posters shown here, graphic designers have used typography to interpret ideas in contemporary architecture. Massimo Vignelli, known for his use of heavy, horizontal bars to organize information, has always allied his work with architecture. In the mid-1980s, Vignelli's partner, Michael Bierut, created several posters that employed typography to illustrate the disintegration of rational modernist structures. William Longhauser's 1983 poster for a lecture by Michael Graves attempted to translate the architect's decorative style into typographic elements. At Cranbrook in the early 80s, the architect Daniel Libeskind was key in the dissemination of post-structuralist theory among graphic designers. Katherine McCoy's poster for the architecture program at Cranbrook includes a text that has been splintered into a field. These posters show that typography, like architecture, can represent ideas through an essentially abstract, non-figurative language.

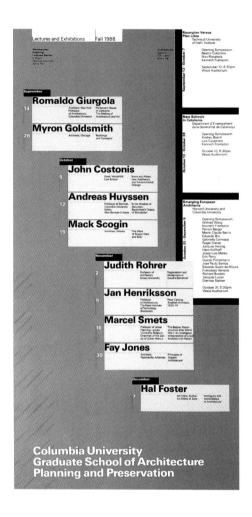

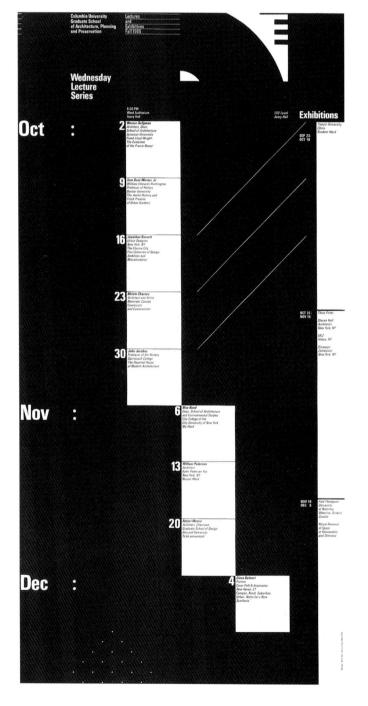

Architecture Lecture Series
Posters, 1985–93, offset lithography
Designer: Willi Kunz (b. 1943)
Publisher: Columbia University,
Graduate School of Architecture,
Planning and Preservation, New York
Collection Cooper-Hewitt, National
Design Museum, Gift of the designer

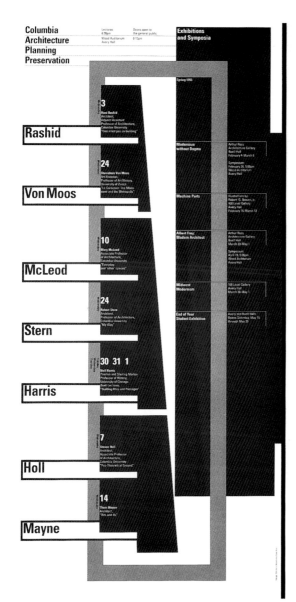

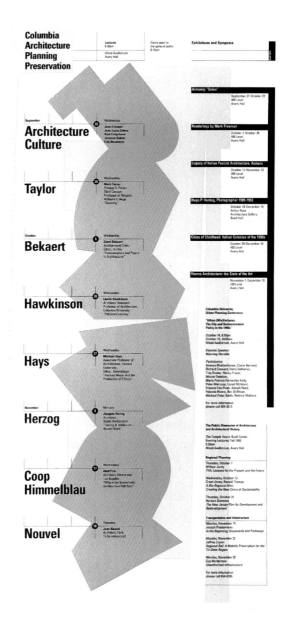

Swiss-born designer Willi Kunz has been producing posters for Columbia University's School of Architecture for over a decade. Comparable to Edward Fella's work for the Detroit Focus Gallery (although totally different in attitude), the series is a rare example of a graphic designer pursuing a project in experimental typography over an extended period of time. Trained in the rigorous Swiss tradition, Kunz participated in the "new typography" that was initiated in the 1970s. His Columbia posters show how a formal language can change and expand even within narrowly defined parameters.

Your Turn, My Turn
Poster, 1983, offset lithograph
Designer: April Greiman (b. 1948)
Publisher: Pacific Design Center,
Los Angeles
Collection Cooper-Hewitt, National
Design Museum, Gift of the designer

California Institute of the Arts
Poster/mailer, 1978, offset lithograph
Designers: Jayme Odgers (b. 1939)
and April Greiman
Publisher: California Institute of the Arts, Valencia
Collection Cooper-Hewitt, National Design Museum

Coop Himmelblau Architects
Stationery, 1990, offset lithograph
Designer: April Greiman
Publisher: Coop Himmelblau Architects,
Los Angeles office
Collection Cooper-Hewitt, National Design
Museum, Gift of the designer

April Greiman is among the most influential
designers to have brought Wolfgang Weingart's
"new typography" to the United States. She added
a passion for color, collage, and pictorial imagery
to Weingart's fascination with unravelling
typographic structures.

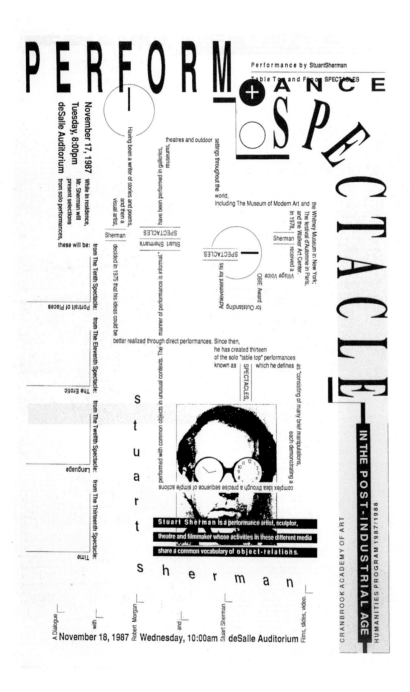

*Performance + Spectacle
in the Post-Industrial Age*
Poster, 1987, offset lithograph
Designer: Allen Hori (b. 1960)
Publisher: Cranbrook Academy
of Art, Bloomfield Hills, Michigan
Collection Cooper-Hewitt,
National Design Museum,
Gift of Katherine McCoy

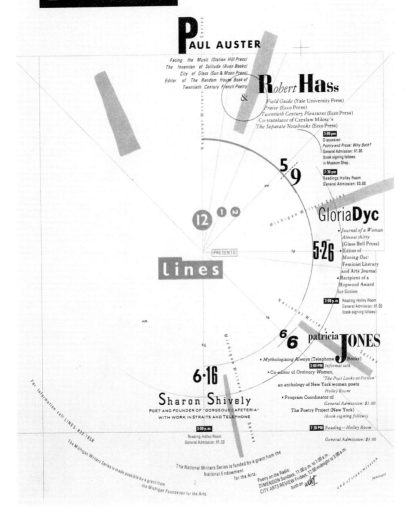

Utne Reader
Magazine, 1995, offset lithograph
Designers: Andrew Henderson (b. 1967)
and Jan Marcus Jancourt
Art director: Andrew Henderson
Publisher: LENS Publishing Co., Inc.,
Minneapolis

Experimental typography initiated at the
Cranbrook Academy has had a broad impact
on design practice, as seen in Jan Marcus
Jancourt's format design for the *Utne
Reader*.

Lines
Poster, 1985, offset lithograph
Designer: Jan Marcus Jancourt (b. 1957)
Publisher: Detroit Institute of Arts
Collection Cooper-Hewitt, National Design
Museum, Gift of Katherine McCoy

In the past, BAM has introduced its audience to JERZY GROTOWSKI, ROBERT WILSON, PETER BROOK, TWYLA THARP. . . Now BAM introduces. . .

PINA BAUSCH and the WUPPERTALER TANZTHEATER have developed a reputation of legendary proportions in sold-out seasons in London, Paris, and the major European arts festivals. The company will open the Olympic Arts Festival in Los Angeles on June 1, 1 9 8 4. T h e following week they will make their N e w Y o r k debut at t h e Brooklyn Academy of Music in what will be t h e season's major performing arts e v e n t. There will be only 12 perform- ances. O n l y 2500 subscribers can be ac- commodated w i t h the best seats. Please order n o w before the engage- ment is sold out.

"Never

PEP

"Every t i m e has its fash- i o n s, and every cultural p e r i o d its g u i d i n g personalities. In new theater this person- ality is PINA BAUSCH. I say 'new theater' . . .to desig- n a t e that theater of movement which looks to the future. . . ."

Artforum

PINA BAUSCH. . . .AN EARTHEN RITE, COLE POR

Brooklyn Academy of Music: Pina Bausch
Poster, 1984, offset lithograph
Designers: Jane Kosstrin (b. 1954)
and David Sterling (b. 1951)
Firm: Doublespace
Publisher: Brooklyn Academy of Music
and Ulli Rose
Collection Cooper-Hewitt, National Design
Museum, Gift of the designers

Jane Kosstrin and David Sterling, graduates of the
Cranbrook Academy of Art, have led influential
careers in New York. Their work for the Brooklyn
Academy of Music in the mid-1980s brought
experimental typography to an audience of
cultural consumers.

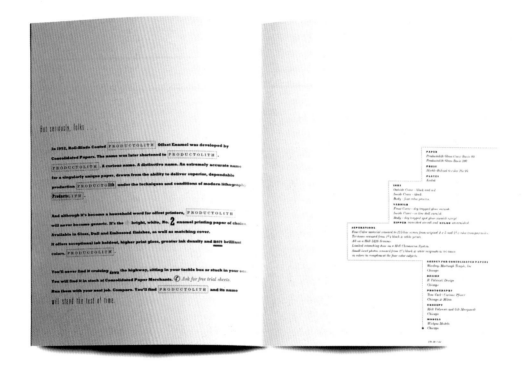

Productolith
Brochure, 1987, offset lithograph
Designer: Rick Valicenti (b. 1951)
Firm: Thirst
Photographers: Tom Vack and Corinne Pfister
Publisher: Consolidated Papers, Inc., Chicago
Collection Cooper-Hewitt, National Design
Museum, Gift of the designer

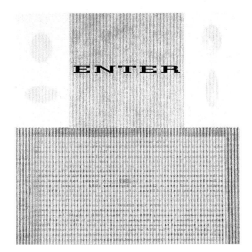

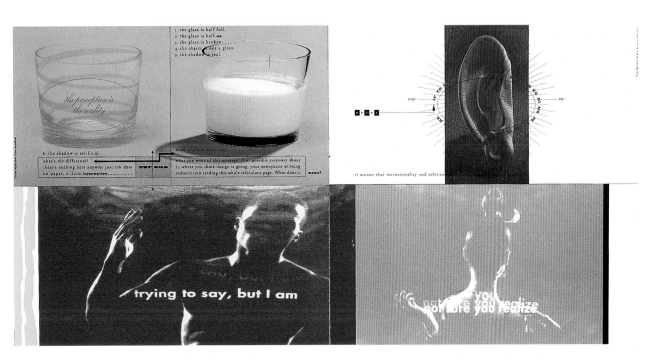

Enter
Brochure, 1989, offset lithograph
Designer: Rick Valicenti
Firm: Thirst
Publisher: Society of Typographic Arts/
American Center for Design, Chicago
Collection Cooper-Hewitt, National Design
Museum, Gift of the designer

Working outside the context of academia,
Rick Valicenti began experimenting with
typography around 1987. His studio, Thirst,
became known for mixing letterforms, symbols,
and illustrations in complex layers.

Art Center College of Design 1991–92
Catalog, 1990, offset lithograph
Designer and art director: Rebeca Méndez (b. 1962)
Assistant designer: Sze Tsung Leong
Creative director: Stuart I. Frolick
Photographers: Steven A. Heller and Eika Aoshima
Publisher: Art Center College of Art and Design, Pasadena
Collection Cooper-Hewitt, National Design Museum,
Gift of the designer

Art Center College of Design 1993-94
Catalog, 1992, offset lithograph
Designer and art director: Rebeca Méndez
Associate designers: Darren Namaye
and Darin Beaman
Creative director: Stuart I. Frolick
Photographer: Steven A. Heller
Publisher: Art Center College of Art and
Design, Pasadena
Collection Cooper-Hewitt, National Design
Museum, Gift of the designer

The publications Rebeca Méndez has designed for the
Art Center College of Art and Design use delicate
layers of image and text that give an atmospheric
quality to the surface of the page.

N A T I O N A L
A E R O N A U T I C S
A N D   S P A C E
A D M I N I S T R A T I O N

NASA HEADQUARTERS
1520 H STREET NORTHWEST
WASHINGTON 25, D. C.
Telephone: EXecutive 3-3260   TWX: WA 755

IN REPLY REFER TO

NASA

National Aeronautics and
Space Administration

Washington, D.C.
20546

Reply to Attn of:

National Aeronautics and
Space Administration
Headquarters
Washington, DC 20546-0001

Reply to Attn of:

NASA letterhead, c. 1959, letterpress
Designer (logo): James Modarelli

NASA letterhead, 1974, offset lithograph
Designer: Danne & Blackburn

NASA letterhead, 1992, offset lithograph
Designer (logo): James Modarelli

Publisher: National Aeronautics Space
Administration, Washington
Collection Cooper-Hewitt, National Design
Museum, Gift of NASA

UFO Weekly
Invitation, 1993, offset lithograph
Designer: Mike Szabo (b. 1971)
Publisher: NASA (Nocturnal Audio Sensory
Awakening), New York
Collection Cooper-Hewitt, National Design
Museum, Gift of the designer

IDENTITY

The central social function of graphic design is to embody identity through visual forms. Design creates a visual personality for institutions, products, audiences, and for designers themselves. Organizations of every size—from multinational conglomerates to corner stores—use design to convey a sense of purpose and a set of values. Typography, icons, color, and other elements symbolize an institution's purpose and services. As a specialized field of design, corporate identity matured in the 1950s, when designers sought to create coherent visual standards that would unify a company's total image. Over the past fifteen years, design for corporate identity has come to favor open, flexible languages over rigid systems. While a corporate mark is a company's private property, once it enters the public realm it is fodder for revision and reuse, becoming part of the broader culture of visual information. Reaching national and international audiences, corporate logos and brand images have generated a literacy of the eye, a commercial alphabet of symbols and styles familiar to participants in consumer culture. Collective identities are visualized not only by businesses and institutions but by communities drawn together around shared political or cultural interests. Activist groups have used design to publicize their commitment to specific issues, from feminism to AIDS, while designers working within the youth cultures of rave, hip-hop, skate-boarding, and snowboarding have evolved visual languages that mix styles and symbols from the mass media and the urban underground. The profession of graphic design is itself a subculture bound by certain myths and symbols. By the end of the 1970s, the design of corporate identity had achieved the appearance of a perfected system. The field had helped legitimize graphic design, elevating the profession's social and economic status with its formal research methods and high-paying, high-profile clients. In the 1980s, the design profession experienced an identity crisis, as practitioners challenged the profession's authority and looked outside its established walls for aesthetic inspiration and social models. Many designers objected to how the restrictive visual grammars and narrow social role of corporate identity had come to dominate the values of the profession.

CORPORATE
CULTURES

Corporate identity design, which took shape in the 1950s, aims to unite an often incongruous mix of people and products in a collective fictional personality. In 1959, a writer for *Advertising Age* described the corporation as being "just as subject to neuroses and inner searchings and optimism and depression...as any single person."[1] Popular theories of psychotherapy flourished in the 50s, when the analyst Erik Erikson coined the term "identity crisis," and the corporation emerged as a new type of troubled individual for whom designers and public relations experts could provide diagnoses and cures. Paul Rand employed geometric icons and clean typography to generate coherent visual codes for IBM, Westinghouse, and other large companies. Design consultancies such as Lippincott & Margulies, whose clients in the 50s included Johnson's Wax and Betty Crocker, brought modernism to the grocery shelf.

The annual report, another tool of corporate identity, burgeoned in the 1950s and 1960s beyond its minimal legal obligation to announce profits and losses into a lavishly produced vehicle for corporate image.[2] By 1980, large companies were putting significant amounts of money into producing these publications. Today, American businesses spend around $4 billion a year producing annual reports.[3] Indeed, their role in conveying financial data has become secondary to their task of expressing corporate identity.

Westinghouse
Logo, 1960
Designer: Paul Rand
(b. 1914)

Betty Crocker
Logo, 1954
Designer:
Lippincott & Margulies

1. Howard Gossage, "Give Your Company a Clear Consistent Identity, and its Advertising Will be Easier, Better," *Advertising Age* (March 9, 1959): 55. *Print* devoted its May/June 1957 issue to corporate identity. See also "Four Major Corporate Design Programs," *Print* 14, 6 (November/December 1960): 31-50.

For current theory, see Wally Olins, *Corporate Identity* (Cambridge: Harvard Business School Press, 1989); and Clive Chajet, *Image by Design* (Reading: Addison-Wesley, 1991).
2. *A Historical Review of Annual Report Design* (New York: Cooper-Hewitt Museum, 1988).

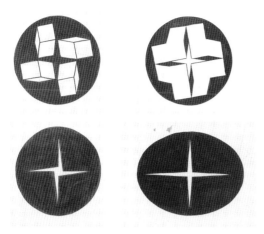

Citibank
Designs for logo, 1975, ink
Designer: Dan Friedman (1945-1995)
Art director: Gene Grossman (b. 1929)
Firm: Anspach Grossman Portugal Inc.
Client: Citibank, New York
Collection Cooper-Hewitt, National Design
Museum, Gift of the Estate of Dan Friedman

The field of corporate identity reached full flower in the 1970s, when consultants became increasingly successful at promoting the economic value of total identity programs to business executives. Writing at the close of the decade, critic Valerie Brooks suggested that design in the 70s had been dominated by corporate values. The principles of consistency and objectivity promoted by corporate design consultants had eclipsed artistic impulses for self-expression and humor; this stiff sobriety extended beyond corporate communications into such areas as advertising and editorial design.[4]

Citibank Identity Manual
Logo, 1975, offset lithograph
Designer: Dan Friedman
Art Director: Gene Grossman
Firm: Anspach Grossman Portugal, Inc.
Collection Cooper-Hewitt, National
Design Museum, Gift of the Estate of
Dan Friedman

The grip of institutional blandness was loosened by the visual program created for Citibank by the New York consultancy Anspach Grossman Portugal in 1975. Senior designer Dan Friedman and art director Gene Grossman brought elements of Wolfgang Weingart's "new typography" to a vast system of signs and printed matter. Following an established strategy in corporate identity design, Friedman and his colleagues reduced the company's existing logo to a minimal mark. In the logo's three-dimensional applications, Friedman introduced a gentle convex curve across the surface of the sign, giving it a sensual, bodily presence. Applying the mark to brochures, forms, and other printed matter, Friedman used grid systems and typographic rules in a playful manner.

85

Citibank
Logo redesign, 1975

3. Michael Rock, "Annual Reports: Corporate Face-Lift or Smoke Screen?" *I.D.* 39 (November/December 1992): 26-28.
4. Valerie F. Brooks, "Triumph of the Corporate Style: Communications Design in the 1970s," *Print* 34, 1 (January/February 1980): 25-47.

Bell
Logo, 1969
Designer: Saul Bass (1920-1996)
Firm: Bass & Yager

AT&T
Logo, 1984
Designer: Saul Bass
Firm: Bass & Yager

Nortel
Logo, 1995, two-dimensional and
three-dimensional versions
Designer and art director:
Will Ayres (b. 1958)
Photographer: Ed Gajdel
Firm: Siegel & Gale

The ability to successfully integrate subtle and complex forms into the field of corporate identity was a triumph for proponents of the new typography, but it was also a disturbing indication that a vanguard sensibility could be appropriated by the profession's culturally conservative center. Friedman abandoned his practice in graphic design in the early 1980s in favor of making experimental furniture that rejected and even ridiculed corporate values of uniformity and control.

Meanwhile, across the corporate landscape fortunes were rapidly built and buried in the midst of the dramatic mergers and divestitures of the 1980s. A prominent symbol of the era was produced for AT&T by the Los Angeles firm Bass & Yager following AT&T's breakup in 1984. The same design firm had created the famous bell symbol for the nationwide phone monopoly in the late 1960s. This icon—which achieved a remarkable 93 percent recognition rate in the United States—aspired to the simplicity and directness of a sans serif letterform. In 1984, the familiar bell symbol was transferred to the divested "Baby Bells," and Bass & Yager designed a striated sphere for AT&T, aiming to signify the corporation's international stature and the ascendence of digital communications.[5]

Striped and streamlined globes had become a weary archetype by the end of the 1980s. Since then, several design firms have tried to reinvest the empty sphere with specificity and depth, generating forms that acknowlege that global communication engages human contact as well as universal infrastructures. In 1990, Lippincott & Margulies designed an

5. On AT&T's identity, see Philip B. Meggs, "Saul Bass on Corporate Identity," *AIGA Journal of Graphic Design* 8, 1 (1990): 4-5; and Paul Sargent Clark, "Ringing the Corporate Bell," *Design* 436 (April 1985): 25.
6. See *Global Corporate Identity* (Rockport, MA: Rockport Publications, 1995).

Continental Airlines
Corporate identity redesign, 1990
Designer: Lippincott & Margulies

identity program for Continental Airlines that replaced the circle-cum-runway logo the company had used since the 1970s. The earlier program featured blandly futuristic typography and an abstracted symbol, presented in cheerful colors that invoked holiday pleasures. The new globe, rendered in blue, gold, and white, is a dignified yet painterly image geared to business travelers.[6]

Siegel & Gale created an image for Nortel (formerly Northern Telecom) in 1995 that revolves around an elegant and ambiguous planetary orb. The Nortel sphere, constructed from a limited set of curves, oscillates between typographic flatness and an illusion of deep space.

The globe, a recurring symbol for the universal reach of business, can also signal ideas of diversity and ecology. The planet Earth, rendered in blue and green, dominates the popular iconography of environmentalism, while trademarks for fashion and sportswear companies designed by Rick Valicenti and Mark Fox put the earth at the center of a highly individualized universe.

Debuting in the same year as AT&T's striped sphere was Prudential Insurance Company of America's striped rock, an extreme simplification of the Rock of Gibraltar drawings

TOP
900 N
Logo, 1987
Designer: Rick Valicenti
Firm: Thirst
Art director: John Jay
Client: Bloomingdale's

MIDDLE
Planet Reebok
Logo proposal, 1992
Designer: Mark Fox (b. 1961)
Firm: BlackDog
Client: Planet Reebok

BOTTOM
Planet Earth
Generic symbol of
the ecology movement
and green marketing

*Prudential Insurance
Company of America*

Logo, concept introduced 1896
Designer unknown

Logo redesign, 1984
Designers: Lee and Young

Logo redesign, 1989
Designer: Kristie Williams (b. 1953)
Art director: Ann Breaznell
Firm: Siegel & Gale

that had symbolized the company since 1896. Retreating from its severely streamlined rock, Prudential introduced a new version in 1989, designed by Siegel & Gale, which returned to a more conventional depiction of the rock. Critic Maud Lavin has linked the rejection of Prudential's sleekly abstract logo, grounded in the futuristic modernism of the 1970s, to the nostalgic "new traditionalism" that gripped the Reagan/Bush era.[7] According to designer Kristie Williams, consumers did not recognize the striped rock as Prudential's symbol. Siegel & Gale's Rock is an immediately understandable pictorial image that subtly conforms with modernist principles of representation: it uses straight lines and a simple pattern of black and white to depict the object through minimal means.[8]

The ability to mix the simple, unornamented forms favored by modernism with culturally legible content is seen in logos designed by Woody Pirtle. Working in Dallas in the 1970s and 1980s before joining the New York office of Pentagram in 1988, Pirtle has brought a sense of humor to the field of corporate identity, designing symbols that are funny and figurative as well as assertively two-dimensional.

Such witty hieroglyphics might prove too specific for a corporation whose reach borders on the infinite. One of the most spectacular corporate consolidations of the late 1980s resulted from the acquisition of Warner Communications by Time, Inc., in which the flashy, West Coast stylishness of Warner confronted the Ivy League, East Coast traditionalism of Time. In 1990, Time Warner commissioned Chermayeff & Geismar Inc. to symbolize the massive new conglomerate with a logo that would reconcile the company's clash of cultures.

Landa Pharmaceutical (1985)

Travis Construction logo (1985)

Fine Line Features (1992)

Logos designed by
Woody Pirtle (b. 1944)

7. Maud Lavin, "The New Tradition-alism and Corporate Identity," *Artforum* 28 (October 1989): 17-19. See also Rose DeNeve, "What Ever Happened to Corporate Identity?" *Print* 43, 3 (May/June 1989): 92-98.

8. Kristie Williams, interview with author, New York, April 1995. Williams, senior designer at Siegel & Gale, studied design at the Kunstgewerbeschule in Basel during the 1980s.

Among the proposed designs was an evocative icon that merged a schematic eye with a spiraling interpretation of an ear. Designer Steff Geissbuhler commented on his design shortly after its release:

> Warner is primarily entertainment, Time is essentially journalism. So a common denominator needed to be much broader: looking and listening, reading and hearing, receiving and sending....I believe the time has come to bring back more symbolic marks when possible and appropriate, because we've been oversaturated with abstractions and letterforms....
> Of course, all this has to be reviewed in a year or two, and then we'll see if we were right.[9]

In 1993, Time Warner replaced the evocative eye/ear symbol with a neutral typographic treatment of the company's name; Chermayeff & Geismar's unusual symbol proved too strong a statement for Time Warner, a vast conglomerate that encompasses numerous separate brand identities having their own distinctive visual marks. The hieroglyph is now used only to identify Time Warner Cable.

The eye/ear logo premiered a few weeks after the publication of Time Warner's 1989 annual report, designed by Frankfurt Gips Balkind, a design and advertising firm with offices in New York and Los Angeles. Provocatively titled *Why?* the annual report was greeted in the press as a surprising new approach to business communications that mixed the visual languages of mass culture with corporate communications.[10] Reflecting the influence of *Spy* and other magazines, the designers favored icons, photographs, and chunks of commentary over running text. They translated

Time Warner
Logo, 1990
Designer and art director:
Steff Geissbuhler (b. 1942)
Firm: Chermayeff & Geismar Inc.

Time Warner 1989 Annual Report
Annual report, 1990, offset lithograph
Designers: Kent Hunter (b. 1956) and
Ricki Sethiadi (b. 1960)
Creative directors: Aubrey Balkind
(b. 1944) and Kent Hunter
Photographers: Scott Morgan and
Geoff Kern
Firm: Frankfurt Gips Balkind
Publisher: Time Warner Inc., New York
Collection Cooper-Hewitt, National
Design Museum, Gift of Frankfurt
Balkind Partners

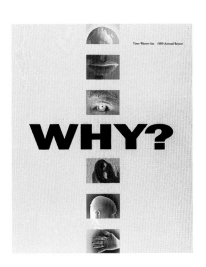

89

9. Steff Geissbuhler, "Making A Mark," *AIGA Journal of Graphic Design* 8, 2 (1990): 12. See also Steff Geissbuhler, "(Eye)/Ear Today—Gone Tomorrow," ibid., 12, 1 (1994): 8.

10. Kim Foltz, "Bored by Annual Reports? Try Time Warner's," *New York Times,* April 4, 1990.

Harley-Davidson® et ses produits sont représentés par différentes versions de logos qui viennent s'ajouter au logo officiel Bar & Shield sans le remplacer pour autant.

La version du Bar & Shield qui inclut un aigle ne constitue pas un logo officiel : elle ne sert que de décoration, dont les applications spécifiques comprennent notamment les T-shirts et accessoires de moto. Ménager un espace libre minimum équivalent à la hauteur du «H» de «Harley» autour du logo de l'aigle et ne placer aucun élément typographique ou graphique dans le rayon spécifié.

Sans être le logo officiel, Harley-Davidson convient parfaitement à toute communication marketing de format horizontal, notamment aux titres de revues. Il peut être également utilisé lors d'activités de sponsoring, notamment lors de l'intervention d'autres sociétés et si Harley souhaite limiter l'usage du Bar & Shield. L'espace libre autour de la marque est fonction du «H» de «Harley» et aucun élément typographique ou graphique ne peut être placé dans le rayon spécifié.

Dorénavant, tous les produits sous licence officielle sont indiqués par un encadré rectangulaire, qui contient les mots «Harley-Davidson». Ce logo indique le statut officiel du produit et la source de l'autorisation sur tous les produits sous licence officielle. Les produits utilisant ce logo sont surveillés de très près dans le but de maintenir un contrôle étroit de l'image de marque. Comme pour les autres logos, un espace libre fonction de la hauteur du «H» de «Harley» fait ressortir le logo. Aucun élément typographique ou graphique ne peut être placé dans le rayon ainsi spécifié. Ce logo remplace son prédécesseur Bar & Shield, portant les mots Motor Cycles accompagné d'un élément en forme de flèche. Ce logo est encore en circulation mais il est progressivement éliminé et Motor Company en restreint donc considérablement l'usage.

Harley-Davidson® and its products are represented by a range of logo treatments that augment but do not substitute for the official Bar & Shield logo.

The version of the Bar & Shield that includes an eagle is for decorative use and is not an official logo. Specific applications include T-shirts and motorcycle accessories. Keep a minimum clear space of the "H" height in "Harley" on all sides of the Eagle logo. Do not place typography or any design element closer than this designated distance.

The Harley-Davidson wordmark, though not an official logo, is appropriate for horizontal format marketing communications, including mastheads. It can also be used when sponsoring events, especially when the sponsorship is in conjunction with other organizations and Harley wants to restrict use of the Bar & Shield. The wordmark's area of isolation is based on the "H" in "Harley." Do not place typography or any design element closer than this designated distance.

From this point forward, all Official Licensed Products are designated by a framed rectangle that encloses the words "Harley-Davidson." This logo indicates both the official standing of the product and the source of authorization on all official licensed products. Products using this logo are monitored rigorously to maintain tight control of the brand image. As with the other logos, an area of isolation, based on the height of the "H" in "Harley," allows the logo to command visual attention. No typography or design element may be placed closer than this designated distance. This logo supercedes the pre-existing Bar & Shield bearing the words Motor Cycles with an arrow-shaped placket. While you may still see this logo, it is being phased out, and therefore its use is highly restricted by the Motor Company.

N'apporter aucune modification et ne faire aucune substitution aux mots Harley-Davidson® Motor Cycles présents dans le Bar & Shield.

Do not make alterations to, or substitutions for, the words Harley-Davidson® Motor Cycles contained within the Bar & Shield.

Ne pas utiliser le logo ordinaire si le logo Bar & Shield est reproduit sur fond noir. Il existe un logo Bar & Shield dans un cadre blanc, spécialement créé à cet effet, et qui se trouve dans les pages graphiques pouvant être reproduites.

Do not use regular logo art when reproducing the Bar & Shield on a black field. A special Bar & Shield contained within a white frame has been created for this purpose and is included in the pages of reproducible art.

Ne pas altérer les couleurs du logo Bar & Shield.

Do not alter the colors of the Bar & Shield.

Ne pas entourer le logo Bar & Shield d'une autre forme.

Do not confine the Bar & Shield within a shape.

Ne pas utiliser d'autre orange que l'orange Harley® (PMS 165) ou son équivalent.

Do not use any orange other than Harley® Orange (PMS 165) or its equivalent.

Ne pas appliquer le logo Bar & Shield sur des fonds susceptibles de détourner l'attention du logo.

Do not apply the Bar & Shield to visually competitive backgrounds.

Ne rien changer aux proportions du logo Bar & Shield.

Vous ne pouvez pas permettre à d'autres personnes d'utiliser les marques de la société.

Do not tamper with the proportions of the Bar & Shield.

You do not have the authority to authorize others to use any of the trademarks of the Company.

Harley-Davidson Global Communications Guidelines
Corporate identity manual, 1993, offset lithograph
Designers: Kenneth Cooke (b. 1947) and Sondra Adams (b. 1963)
Art director: Kenneth Cooke
Firm: Siegel & Gale
Publisher: Harley-Davidson Inc., Milwaukee
Collection Cooper-Hewitt, National Design Museum, Gift of Siegel & Gale

dense pages of financial information into a double-page spread of charts and graphs, peppered with photographs of Madonna and Bugs Bunny. According to partner Aubrey Balkind, "We took things from surf culture, fashion, and media, and we brought them into corporate communications. We don't claim to have invented anything new, but we brought these forms into a new place."[11]

Time Warner's 1989 annual report exemplified the ability of a major corporation to project an image of its own culture by absorbing the languages of smaller ones. The concept of "corporate culture"—a set of shared attitudes ranging from dress codes and taste in furniture to meeting styles, lines of power, and patterns of decision-making—has gained increasing prestige in the professional parlance of image management. In a 1991 promotional booklet, Frankfurt Gips Balkind predicted the convergence of corporate communications with mainstream media and argued that a company would benefit from including a mix of "counter-cultures" in its overall framework rather than aspiring to express a single, monolithic personality.[12] Such developments have been praised as a progressive recognition of diversity and critiqued as a process that deadens differences by converting them into commodities.

The corporate communications of Harley-Davidson Inc. have negotiated nimbly between the different cultures the company serves, from bikers and Harley employees to the financial community. The company's 1993 *Global Communications Guidelines*, created by Siegel & Gale, makes light of the restrictions such guides enforce. A standards manual is

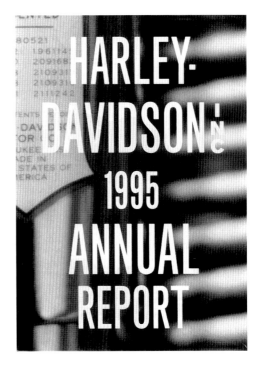

Harley-Davidson Inc 1995 Annual Report
Annual report, 1995, offset lithograph
Art directors: Dana Arnett (b. 1960) and Curtis Schreiber (b. 1967)
Photographer: James Schnepf
Firm: VSA Partners, Inc.
Publisher: Harley-Davidson Inc., Milwaukee

11. Kent Hunter and Aubrey Balkind, interview with author, New York, July 1994. See also Robert A. Parker, "Frankfurt Gips Balkind," *Communication Arts* (September/October 1991): 24-37.

12. Frankfurt Gips Balkind, *Culture and Corporations* (San Francisco: Simpson Paper Company, 1991). Recent articles on "corporate culture" include Patricia Buhler, "Managing in the 90s," *Supervision* 54, 9 (September 1993): 17-9; and Tom Atwood, "Corporate Culture: For or Against You?" *Management Accounting* 68, 1 (January 1990): 26-29.

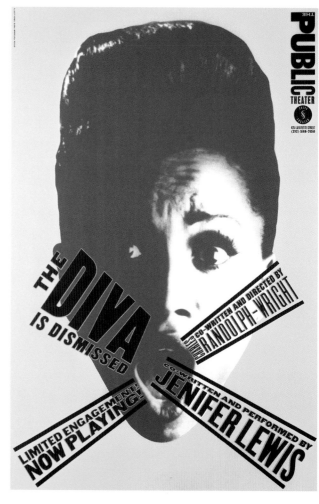

Shakespeare Varieties
Poster, 1960s, letterpress
Designer unknown, Liverpool

Simpatico
Poster, 1994, silkscreen

The Diva is Dismissed
Poster, 1994, silkscreen

Designer: Paula Scher (b. 1948)
Firm: Pentagram
Publisher: The Public Theater, New York
Collection Cooper-Hewitt, National
Design Museum, Gift of the designer

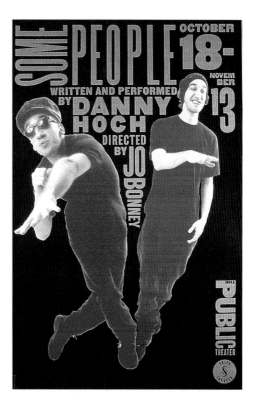

the philosophical scripture of an identity program. By the 1970s, these manuals had become massive, elaborately printed documents presented in imposing binders, replete with specifications for the correct use of logos, colors, typefaces, signs, and so on. In Harley's *Guidelines,* a skull-and-crossbones lurks with mock ominousness behind a series of forbidden variants of the company's logo. Since 1991, VSA Partners, located in Chicago, has produced Harley-Davidson's annual reports; designer Dana Arnett has employed thin shiny paper, heavy black typography, big biker photos, and a judicious use of gold to convey the culture of Harley.

In 1994, the New York Public Theater transformed its visual identity, and the streets of the city, with a program of posters, flyers, banners, and other paraphernalia designed by Paula Scher at Pentagram. From large-scale billboards down to the logo and stationery, the theater's image is expressed in a rhythmic mix of letterforms. Sans serif type runs in various directions in contrasting scales, fitted together like the pieces of a puzzle. Scher's approach recalls vernacular theater posters and tickets that carve the available space into zones and then fill them to the brim.[13] Simon Johnston's 1992 work for LACE (Los Angeles Contemporary Exhibitions) takes the idea of mixed identity in another direction by printing stationery on the backs of billboard sheets and showcards. Each piece, cut from a different source, is unique.

Designers visualize the character of innumerable organizations, from global businesses to local theaters and museums. Design for institutions has come to embrace values of complexity over simplicity, as restrictive systems have made way for open grammars and legible icons.

Some People
Poster, 1994, silkscreen
Designer: Paula Scher (b. 1948)
Firm: Pentagram
Publisher: The Public Theater, New York
Collection Cooper-Hewitt, National Design Museum, Gift of the designer

LACE
Envelope, 1992, mixed media
Designer: Simon Johnston (b. 1959)
Firm: Praxis
Client: LACE (Los Angeles Contemporary Exhibitions)
Collection Cooper-Hewitt, National Design Museum, Gift of the designer

93

13. Steven Heller, "Street Theater," *Print* 50, 3 (May/June 1996): 29-35.

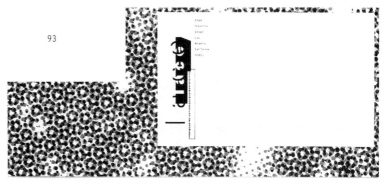

Smells Like Smoked Sausages
Album cover, 1992, offset lithograph
Designer: Art Chantry (b. 1954)
Art director: Tom Hazelmeyer/Amphetamine Reptile
Publisher: Sub Pop Records, Seattle
Collection Cooper-Hewitt, National Design Museum,
Gift of Art Chantry

Buzzmuscle: Assembler
Album cover (front and back), 1991,
offset lithograph
Conception, design and copy:
Rob Warmowski (b. 1967)
Design, photography, production:
Greg Dunlap (b. 1968)
Logo: Lisa M. Owen
Additional production: Mark Evans
Publisher: Jake Records
Collection Cooper-Hewitt, National
Design Museum, Gift of Barefoot Press

Tsunami: In a Name
Album cover, 1993, offset lithograph
Designer: Steve Raskin (b. 1968)
and John Pamer (b. 1971)
Art director: Steve Raskin
Firm: Ion Design, Washington, DC
Collection Cooper-Hewitt, National
Design Museum, Gift of Steve Raskin

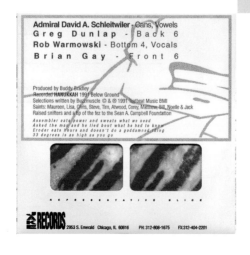

SUBCULTURES

A culture can be as narrow as a supermarket circular or as broad as the national news. There is no single culture in the United States, but rather a vast web of overlapping mass cultures and subcultures, organized around class, race, geography, generation, profession, and other affiliations. Graphic design expresses cultural identity by creating symbols and styles that become associated with particular groups. The languages of identity, applied to products, packaging, publishing, and fashion often mix visual elements from different sources. The commercial vocabulary of mass consumption is familiar to a broad, nearly universal audience. This common language provides fertile ground for spawning new identities aimed at narrower groups.

The entertainment industry, dominated by such corporate giants as Time Warner and Disney, includes many independent producers and distributors as well. These companies often work with visual languages that emerge out of the communities of artists and consumers who make and use their products. Art Chantry's poster and package designs for the Seattle music industry merge mass culture with street life. Kristin Thomson and Jenny Toomey, who own the music label Simple Machines in Arlington, Virginia, are also that company's chief graphic designers. Barefoot Press, a printing plant in Raleigh, North Carolina, produces packages for numerous independent labels, often working directly with musical artists who serve as their own designers.

Liquor Giants: You're Always Welcome
Album cover, 1992, offset lithograph
Designer: Art Chantry
Publisher: Jay Haskins/Lucky Records, Seattle
Collection Cooper-Hewitt, National Design
Museum, Gift of the designer

95

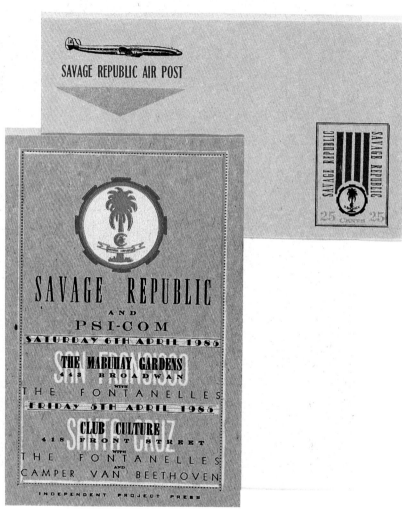

Independent Project Press and *Savage Republic*
Stationery, 1986–1992, letterpress
Designer: Bruce Licher (b. 1958)
Publisher: Independent Project Press, Sedona, Arizona
Collection Cooper-Hewitt, National Design Museum,
Gift of Independent Project Press

Independent Project Press, located in Sedona, Arizona, was established by Bruce Licher in 1984 to produce packaging and graphics for his own band, Savage Republic. The press was soon doing work for other groups attracted to Licher's seductively tactile use of hand-set wood and metal type, printed on industrial materials. Licher's visual identity for Savage Republic includes not only a logo but stamps, banknotes, and flags, the visual trappings of a mythic nation in which raw primitivism converges with civilized democracy.

In the late 1980s and early 1990s, a new genre of music ephemera was spawned by "raves," large dance parties staged at remote industrial sites. By 1993, raves, which originated in Manchester, England, were a national phenomena in the United States, where promoters translated clandestine parties into more commercial forms of entertainment. The music for raves is made by disk jockeys who mix together existing recordings. Mike Szabo, a designer connected with the New York rave known as NASA, explained, "The music at raves is live. Although the source for the music is prerecorded, a disk jockey working at a mixing table is performing new music for a live audience."[14]

This aesthetic of mixing informs the distinctive graphics that promote raves. The designers of these palm-sized posters use desktop equipment to manipulate existing images and typefaces. Rave designers typically combine material from ads, stock photos, television, comic books, commercial packaging, and other sources, often producing a final design within a few hours and providing printers with films or electronic files for immediate production.

Tsumami: Be Like That Newspaper
Album cover, 1993, offset lithograph
Designer: Kristin Thomson (b. 1967)
Publisher: Simple Machines, Arlington, Virginia
Collection Cooper-Hewitt, National Design
Museum, Gift of Simple Machines

Shellac: The Bird is the Most Popular Finger
Album cover, 1993, offset lithograph
Designers: Steve Albini (b. 1962), Bob Weston
(b. 1965) and Todd Trainer (b. 1963)
Firm: Shellac of North America
Publisher: Drag City, Chicago
Collection Cooper-Hewitt, National Design
Museum, Gift of Steve Albini

97

14. Mike Szabo, interview with author and Paul Makovsky, New York, August 1994. On rave graphics see Michael Dooley, "Frequent Flyers," *Print* (March/April 1993): 42-53; and Peter Tulupman, "Rave Exhibit," *Project X* 28 (spring 1994): 34-35.

For evidence of the popularity of raves, see Edna Gundersen, "Hyperkinetic Techno Music Wins Dance Floor Raves," *USA Today*, December 4, 1992.

Soap

Saturdays USA

Cream of the Crop

Invitations, 1994, offset lithograph
Designers unknown, New York

Nasooka
Invitation, 1993, offset lithograph
Designer: Mike Szabo
Art directors: Scotto and D. B.
Publisher: NASA (Nocturnal Audio
Sensory Awakening), New York
Collection Cooper-Hewitt, National
Design Museum, Gift of the designer

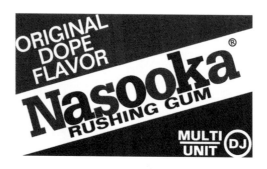

"R," Mob, OD
Logo revisions, 1994
Designer: Tom McGlynn (b. 1958)

Kids Club
Poster, 1990, silkscreen
Designer: Doug Minkler (b. 1949)
Client: Doctors Ought to Care, Houston
Collection Cooper–Hewitt, National
Design Museum, Gift of the designer

The designers of rave flyers have frequently parodied the brand identities of well-known consumer goods, tapping the energy of the familiar to promote an underground, quasi-secret, event. Rick Klotz, who founded the Los Angeles company Fresh Jive Graphics in 1990, is credited with triggering rave culture's widespread borrowing of national trademarks and brand images with his flyer *Truth*, based on the Tide detergent box. This strategy is indebted, of course, to Pop art, rediscovered by a younger generation fascinated with the ability to use the aggressive iconography of commercial life to convey the attitude of a subculture.

For his unsigned New York band Lotion, Tony Zajkowski converted a series of national brand names into logos for his own group, pasting them on walls and construction fences in 1991.

Artist Tom McGlynn has taken a different approach. To produce a series of T-shirt designs in 1994, he revised and reassembled well-known corporate identities to reveal new messages that are contained, like puzzles, within the original. The anti-smoking posters of Doug Minkler turn elements of familiar packages into grotesque parodies. The political critique expressed in these projects is absent, in most cases, from the irreverent but joyful quotations made in the youth cultures of raves and hip-hop.

99

Lotion
Logos, 1991
Designer: Tony Zajkowski (b. 1966)
Publisher: Lotion, New York

Deee-Lite: Infinity Within
CD package, 1992, offset lithograph
Designer: Mike Mills (b. 1966)
Art directors: Mike Mills and Lady Kier
Photographers: Joshua Jordan and
Patrik Andersson
Publisher: Elektra Entertainment, New York
Collection Cooper-Hewitt, National
Design Museum, Gift of the designer

Global Ghetto
Drawing, 1994, marker
Designer: Mike Mills

Deee-Lite: I Had a Dream
CD package, 1992, offset lithograph
Designer: Mike Mills
Art directors: Mike Mills and Lady Kier
Photographer: Joshua Jordan
Publisher: Elektra Entertainment, New York
Collection Cooper-Hewitt, National
Design Museum, Gift of the designer

Supreme
Sticker, 1994, offset lithograph
Designer: James Jebbia (b. 1963)
Publisher: Supreme, New York

IDENTITY

Such borrowings of institutional identities treat the symbols of corporate culture as public property open to reuse. National brand images constitute a second alphabet, a vocabulary of visual symbols that people instinctively recognize. By mixing familiar forms with new messages, designers bank on the way this second alphabet has been internalized in the collective psyche of consumers.

Brand images—invented and borrowed—are an important feature of the subcultures revolving around skateboarding and snowboarding. Various artifacts express the social milieu of these sports, from boards, hats, and T-shirts to fanzines, magazines, and commercial catalogs. Since the late 1980s, the skateboard industry has largely consisted of small, skater-owned companies who use members of their own skateboard teams to design product graphics. Mike Mills, a skateboarder and graphic designer, has described the transformation of skateboarding from a primarily white, suburban sport in the 1960s and 1970s to a multiracial urban phenomenon in the 1980s and 1990s: "Skating's crossover to urban kids of color is part of a larger mixing between white kids listening to rap, rap musicians such as Ice-T playing heavy metal...and the cross influence between the New York homeboy and California skate/surf fashions." Mills described the hijacking of mainstream corporate logos as a "new critical materialism"—a reaction against the anti-consumer ethos of punk—that embraces a cycle of rapidly changing styles and symbols.

Poot!
Sticker, 1994, offset lithograph
Designer: Keva Marie
Publisher: Foundation Super Co.,
San Diego

Toy Machine Panties!
Garment label, 1994, fabric
Designer: Keva Marie
Publisher: Foundation Super Co.,
San Diego

Foundation Super Co.
Sticker, 1994, offset lithograph
Designer: Tod Swank (b. 1966)
Publisher: Foundation Super Co.,
San Diego

101

FOUNDATION SUPER CO.

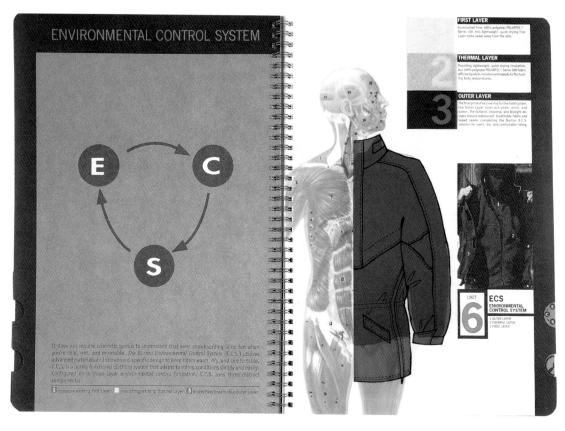

Burton Marmot
Dealer catalog, 1994, offset lithograph
Designers: David Covell (b. 1965) and
Keith Brown (b. 1970)
Creative directors: Michael Jager (b. 1965)
and David Covell

Publisher: Burton Snowboards,
Burlington, Vermont
Collection Cooper-Hewitt, National Design
Museum, Gift of Jager Di Paola Kemp

blur
Magazine, 1994, offset lithograph
Designer: Scott Clum (b. 1964)
Firm and publisher: ride Design
Collection Cooper-Hewitt, National
Design Museum, Gift of the designer

IDENTITY

While young people living in the suburbs might choose to counter their affluent surroundings with an anti-consumerist stance, acts of conspicuous consumption provide urban young people with signs of status and a means to challenge common stereotypes about their buying power.[15]

The products and graphics of snowboarding lean heavily on the language of the skateboard scene. Snowboarding began as an extension of the sleek, taut sports culture of skiing. After the introduction of freestyle snowboarding—a response to freestyle skateboarding—in the late 1980s, snowboard manufacturers began taking design cues from skateboarding. Designers and studios such as Jager di Paola Kemp in Vermont, Modern Dog in Seattle, Scott Clum in Oregon, and Carlos Segura in Chicago have applied carefully detailed typography, intensive image manipulation, and deluxe printing techniques to trade catalogs for snowboards. Such publications contrast with the crudely made product literature generated by the skateboard industry while employing similar motifs, such as scientific diagrams. Although snowboarding has a street-wise style, it is an expensive sport with luxurious graphics to match.[16]

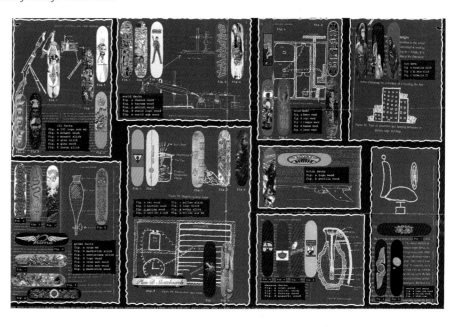

15. Mike Mills, "Which One Doesn't Belong with the Others? The Style and Graphics of Skateboarding," in *Lift and Separate: Design and the Quote Unquote Vernacular*, ed. Barbara Glauber (New York: The Cooper Union, 1993): 48-55.

16. David Covell, designer at Jager di Paola Kemp, interview with author, April 1995; Brett MacFadden, interview with author, New York, February 1995. MacFadden is a snowboard enthusiast.

World Academy Training Manual
Catalog, 1994, offset lithograph
Designer: Steve Rocco
Art director: John Thomas
Photographer: Rick Kosick
Illustrator: Marc McKee
Publisher: World Industries,
El Segundo, California

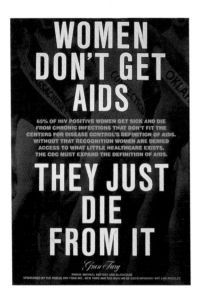

ACT UP, the AIDS Coalition to Unleash Power, was founded in New York in March 1987. The group's logo consists of the phrase "Silence = Death" written over a pink triangle. The triangle recalls the pink tags sewn on the sleeves of homosexuals in Nazi prison camps; by inverting the triangle, the *Silence = Death* symbol aimed to suggest resistance and strength. Rejecting the handmade "outsider" look associated with an earlier generation of political artists, designers working with ACT UP New York created posters, flyers, and other ephemera in a confident style that emulated the authority of advertising and journalism. ACT UP distributed these graphics in conjunction with "actions" performed in public places, from Wall Street to the White House.[17]

WAC, the Women's Action Coalition, was founded in New York in 1992 in response to the Clarence Thomas/Anita Hill Congressional hearings on sexual harrassment. For WAC demonstrations in New York, Washington, Houston, and other cities, Bethany Johns and Marlene McCarty designed posters that amplified the group's image and inspired participation. WAC's logo, emblazoned on T-shirts, buttons, and posters, features a wide-open eye encircled by the slogan, "WAC is Watching/Women Take Action." Like ACT UP's *Silence = Death* symbol, the WAC icon publicized the group and galvanized its members around a shared identity.[18] The considerable media attention earned by ACT UP and WAC during their heights of activity attests to design's ability to provoke action as well as sell products.

17. On ACT UP, see Douglas Crimp and Adam Rolston, *AIDS Demo Graphics* (Seattle: Bay Press, 1990). See also Dan Friedman, "Guerilla Design I: Gran Fury," and Julie Lasky, "Guerrilla Design II: ACT UP," *AIGA Journal of Graphic Design* 8, 2 (1990): 6-7.

18. See Pamela A. Ivinski, "Women Who Turn the Gaze Around," *Print* (December 1993): 36-43; Phoebe Hoban, "Big WAC Attack," *New York Magazine* (August 3, 1992): 31-35; and Karrie Jacobs, "Graphic Action," *I.D.* (November 1992): 42-45.

DESIGN
CULTURES

Silence = Death
Poster, 1986, offset lithograph
Designer and publisher:
Silence = Death Project, New York

Women Don't Get AIDS,
They Just Die from It
Poster, 1991, offset lithograph
Designers: Gran Fury
Posted in bus shelters in
Los Angeles and New York

WAC is Watching
Poster, 1992, offset lithograph
Designer: Marlene McCarty (b. 1957)
Publisher: WAC, Women's Action
Coalition, New York
Collection Cooper-Hewitt, National
Design Museum, Gift of the designer

Hers and Hers
Poster, 1992, diazo print
Designer: Bethany Johns (b. 1956)
Publisher: Women's Action Coalition
(WAC), New York, for the 1992 Gay
Pride March, Washington, DC

Every institution has an image that it projects—deliberately or haphazardly—to its public. These images are shaped by both professional designers and the purveyors of ready-made signs, stationery, and software. A logo or letterhead, whether ordered out of a catalog or commissioned from a design consultant, speaks about the cultural values of its bearer.

Graphic designers create visual identities for groups ranging from vast corporate conglomerates to political and artistic subcultures. Designers also use their work to articulate their own identities as visual producers—whether they define themselves primarily as artists, activists, fans, or members of the profession of graphic design. The profession's official discourse has traditionally defined "design" as a socially enlightened, intellectually self-conscious practice elevated above a broader field of crass commercial production and naive folk art. The center of this official discourse is occupied by corporate identity, a field that has helped confer legitimacy on the broader practice of design.

Graphic designers began rationalizing the standard forms of the magazine, newspaper, shop sign, letterhead, and other commercial genres in the early twentieth century. Yet the distinctive product provided by the profession has not been so much the physical artifacts that it shapes as an elusive aura of visual authority. Graphic designers sell their clients such

Tropi·nasa
PREMIUM RAVE
CONCENTRATED DJ FORCE

100% Pure
Florida Special
NASA JUICE
SUNSHINE POWERED
NET. NYC'S FINEST QUALITY PRODUCTION(1 PINT)

Tropi-nasa Premium Rave
Advertisement, 1993, offset lithograph
Designer: Mike Szabo (b. 1971)
Publisher: NASA (Nocturnal Audio
Sensory Awakening), New York
Collection Cooper-Hewitt, National
Design Museum, Gift of the designer

NASA letterhead, c. 1959, letterpress
Designer (logo): James Modarelli

NASA letterhead, 1974, offset lithograph
Designer: Danne & Blackburn

NASA letterhead, 1992, offset lithograph
Designer (logo): James Modarelli

Publisher: National Aeronautics Space
Administration, Washington
Collection Cooper-Hewitt, National
Design Museum, Gift of NASA

values as stylistic originality, planned rationality, and objective problem-solving, in contrast with the conventional, formulaic effects of "commercial art" and ready-made business ephemera. The history of design as a profession has been shaped by an ongoing struggle to define and defend this aura of visual authority.[19]

"Design culture" consists of a network of schools, studios, magazines, museums, publishers, professional societies, paper companies, and so on. Although all communication takes a physical form, graphic designers, in the professional sense, have not always been part of the process. Designers have had to prove their relevance and find their place among editors, advertisers, printers, marketing specialists, software engineers, public relations experts, and other figures responsible for the look of communications.

While marks such as Paul Rand's logos for IBM and Westinghouse came to symbolize the ascendence of the profession, the values they represented came under attack from several fronts in the 1980s and 1990s. Prudential's retreat from abstraction to illustration in 1989 revealed the fragility of advanced design within corporate culture.

NATIONAL
AERONAUTICS
AND SPACE
ADMINISTRATION

NASA HEADQUARTERS
1520 H STREET NORTHWEST
WASHINGTON 25, D. C.
TELEPHONE: EXECUTIVE 3-3260   TWX: WA 755

IN REPLY REFER TO

NASA
National Aeronautics and
Space Administration

Washington, D.C.
20546

Reply to Attn of:

National Aeronautics and
Space Administration
Headquarters
Washington, DC 20546-0001

Reply to Attn of:

Amazing! New Ideas!
Poster, 1989, silkscreen
Designer: Charles S. Anderson (b. 1958)
and Dan Olson
Art Director: Charles S. Anderson
Illustration: CSA Archive Stock Image
Collection
Publisher: Visual Arts Museum, School
of Visual Arts, New York

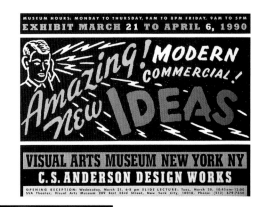

A similar reaction against modernism erupted around Danne & Blackburn's logo for NASA, designed in 1974. The modernist mark, known as the "worm" by people at the space agency, was one of the few graphical triumph's of the Nixon administration's Federal Design Program. The designers abstracted the *A*'s in the word "NASA" into minimal cones that metaphorically suggest rockets ready for take-off. The modernist worm came under fire in 1992 from NASA chief Daniel S. Goldin, who decided to return to the romantic and figurative trademark of 1959 (known at NASA as the "meatball").[20] For Goldin, the older logo represented optimistic days of glory for the space program, an era before the space shuttle disaster: "The can-do spirit of the past is alive and well. The magic is back."[21]

NASA's rearguard, late-Reagan-era battle with the modernist worm coincided with widespread nostalgia within the design profession for conventional commercial idioms and traditional decorative styles. Angered that the polished modernism exemplified by corporate identity had come to dominate the values of their community, designers drew on forms of communication that seemed free from the restrictive norms of corporate identity. The term *vernacular* became a label for visual forms ranging from Victorian fruit-crate labels to standard highway signs.

The Minneapolis firm Duffy Design launched successful revivals of quaint commercial styles beginning in the mid-1980s. Charles S. Anderson, a principle designer in the Duffy group, founded his own studio in 1989. Anderson's and Duffy's revisions of "naive" commercial art from the 1940s and 1950s

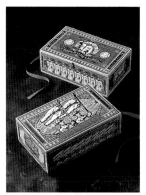

Classico Pasta Sauce
Packaging, 1986–87, glass jar,
offset lithograph label
Designers: Charles S. Anderson
and Haley Johnson
Firm: Joe Duffy Design, Inv.
Client: The International Gourmet Specialties
Company, Pennsauken, New Jersey

Chaps
Corporate promotion, 1987–88, silkscreen
Designer: Joe Duffy (b. 1949)
and Sara Ledgard
Client: Ralph Lauren, New York

19. Ellen Lupton, "Been Down So Long It Looks Like Up to Me," *AIGA Journal of Graphic Design* 10, 3 (1992): 1-2.
20. See Philip B. Meggs, "The Crash of the NASA Logo: It Could Have been Worse!" *AIGA Journal of Graphic Design* 10, 4 (1992): 12-13; and Michael Rock, "Logo Wars: Should NASA Go Back to the Future with Its Visual Identity?" *I.D.* (September/October 1993): 24-26. See also "Designer Reflects on Creation of NASA 'Meatball,' " *Lewis News* 29, 14, NASA in-house publication (July 3, 1992): 1; and "James J. Modarelli Retires," ibid., 16, 2 (January 19, 1979): 1.

21. Glen E. Swanson, "The Meatball is Back! A Look at the Origins of NASA Insignias and Crew Patches," *Quest*, NASA in-house publication (summer 1992): 26-30.

Lost in the Stars: The Music of Kurt Weill
Album cover, 1985, offset lithograph
Designer: Alexander Isley (b. 1961)
Art director: Tibor Kalman (b. 1949)
Firm: M&Co.
Publisher: A+M Records, Hollywood
Collection Cooper-Hewitt, National
Design Museum, Gift of Tibor Kalman

Restaurant Florent
Postcard, 1988, offset lithograph
Designers: Tibor Kalman and Alexander Isley
Firm: M&Co.
Publisher: Restaurant Florent, New York
Collection Cooper-Hewitt, National
Design Museum, Gift of Tibor Kalman

capitalized on the nostalgia that gripped many American consumers during the Reagan/Bush years. Their packaging for Classico pasta sauce uses a glass jar with a screw-top lid and richly illustrated labels to envelope a mass produced product with an image suggesting hand-prepared food.

The New York studio M&Co. pursued its own approach to the vernacular during the 1980s. Founder Tibor Kalman was an outspoken critic of all corners of the design profession, attacking everything from corporate modernism to Duffy's and Anderson's alluring quotations of history. Kalman approached design as an outsider discourse, a medium that can barb as well as serve corporate structures. M&Co. converted the everyday dialect of quick-print wedding typography and felt-board lobby signage into urban chic. The use of icons—from anonymous phone book illustrations to tiny photographs of generic objects—was part of M&Co.'s signature style: pictures became typographic. The use of vernacular forms effaced the hubris of the profession by promoting the absence of art and the disappearance of the designer. While Kalman presented himself as an outsider, his work had a broad cultural impact, with clients including prominent corporations and developers as well as cafes, record companies, and fashion designers.[22]

The word "vernacular" refers in its literal sense to a verbal dialect that is not a community's official language. Before the rise of the printing press, European languages were considered vernacular tongues, in contrast with the official Latin and Greek that was used by literate classes. In the visual arts, vernacular expression includes forms of

22. *Print* magazine organized a debate between Tibor Kalman and Joe Duffy in 1990. Kalman attacked Duffy for using "fake nostalgia," and defended his own work as engaged in the "process" behind vernacular design. "Tibor Kalman vs. Joe Duffy," *Print* 44, 2 (March/April 1990): 68-75. The Duffy/Kalman conflict also was discussed in "Debating Design," *I.D.* (November/December 1990): 29-33.

building, publishing, and signage that reflect local customs and are produced outside the discourse of the state.

The 1994 redesign of Federal Express's public image canonized a phrase from everyday speech. The San Francisco-based consultancy Landor Associates cut the company's name down to FedEx, capitalizing on a piece of international slang that had, through popular use, begun to replace the company's proper name. In contrast with the dramatically shaped and angled letters the company had used since the 1970s, the new logotype employs upright roman letters.[23]

As an institution, design traditionally has defined itself in opposition to commonplace commercial styles and do-it-yourself printing and publishing. Sometimes the vernacular has been despised, and sometimes it has been honored, but in either case it has been seen as the naive, unknowing "other" of the profession.[24]

Consider the work of Globe Poster Printing Corporation, a company that has created music promotions for black communities in the Baltimore/Washington region since 1929. Globe, a job printer, sells design and manufacturing services directly to clients, thus making the professional design consultant unnecessary. Globe's in-house compositor Harry Knorr developed a poster style in the 1950s that featured wood and metal typography printed on top of bright, silkscreened fields of color. After the company switched to digital composition and offset printing in 1988, many of Knorr's signature headlines were replicated in electronic scans. The distinctive look of Globe's posters evolved at a slow, deliberate pace across decades of technological change.

FedEx
Corporate identity redesign, 1994
Art director: Lindon Gray Leader (b. 1949)
Firm: Landor Associates

23. "Why Federal Express Became FedEx," @*issue* 1, 1 (1995): 4-14; and Lynn Baxter, "Self-Expression," *Identity* (July/August 1995): 54-59; 24. On uses of the vernacular, see Barbara Glauber, ed., *Lift and Separate* (New York: The Cooper Union, 1993). See also "Low and High: Design in Everyday Life," in Ellen Lupton and J. Abbott Miller, *Design Writing Research: Writing on Graphic Design* (New York: Kiosk and Princeton Architectural Press, 1996).

Modern Dog
Stationery, 1993, offset lithograph
Designer: Michael Strassburger (b. 1962)
Publisher: Modern Dog, Seattle
Collection Cooper-Hewitt, National Design
Museum, Gift of Modern Dog

Although the direct, unpretentious style of Globe's posters might be deemed a crude "vernacular" by some designers, the posters are viewed as a language of authority by the audience that reads them. According to Ken Moore of Icylce Productions, a company that promotes music events in Washington, "Globe pretty much sets the standard in making the show 'official.' People in the Metro area are conditioned to recognize that, when they see a Globe poster, they know the show is really going on. You see fliers and handbills all the time, but if someone goes to the expense of ordering from Globe and putting up the posters, people feel pretty good that an artist or a group actually is going to be there."[25] Globe posters give credibility to the events that they announce: for the public the posters serve, they are a formal, authoritative presence.

The word *vernacular* is useful for thinking about graphic design insofar as it suggests the existence of visual languages addressing different cultures. But vernacular design should be seen not as a realm beneath and outside "the profession" but as a broad territory whose inhabitants speak a range of local dialects, from the insider codes of skateboard culture to the mass-market hieroglyphics of national brand names. The term vernacular is relative rather than absolute. There exists not one vernacular, but a potentially infinite series of visual languages, of which "mass culture" and "corporate culture" constitute distinct sets of idioms.

111

25. Quoted in Michael Dolan, "How Globe Poster Turned Its World Dayglo," *Washington City Paper,* September 9, 1994.

Statesboro Arena
Poster, c. 1970, silkscreen

North American Tour '94
Poster, 1994, silkscreen

Designer: Globe Poster, Baltimore
Collection Cooper-Hewitt, National
Design Museum, Gift of Globe Poster

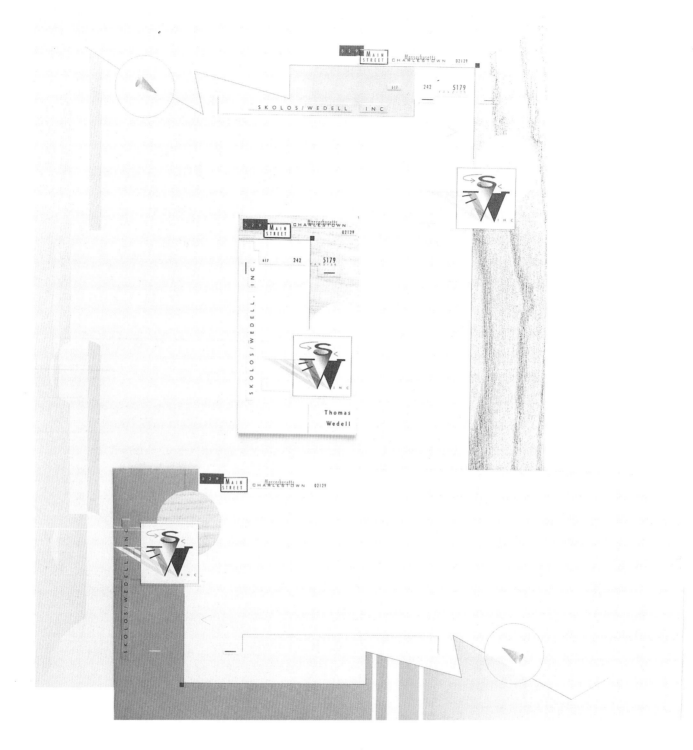

Skolos/Wedell
Stationery, 1990, offset lithograph
Designer: Nancy Skolos (b. 1955)
Publisher: Skolos/Wedell, Boston
Collection Cooper-Hewitt, National Design
Museum, Gift of the designer

The design profession encompasses its own range of subcultures. The stationery programs for two design firms, Modern Dog in Seattle and Skolos/Wedell in Boston, reveal the opposing manners in which designers can choose to represent themselves. The streetwise style of Modern Dog emulates the hard colors and brash typography used in urban music and theater promotions, while Skolos/Wedell's delicately detailed, lavishly produced letterhead design is steeped in the history of the avant-garde, from Cubism to the "new typography" of the 1970s and 1980s.

The languages of corporate cultures, mass cultures, subcultures, and design cultures have become increasingly fluid, with members of each world poaching upon the territory of the others. As corporations see their own internal communities become less homogeneous and centralized, monolithic visual systems are giving way to more accessible and flexible forms. Subcultures supply visual energy to vast media conglomerates and national advertising campaigns while feeding, in turn, on the visual equity of established brand images. Professional designers have found themselves shuttling among these territories. Some continue to search for their own legitimacy in the field of corporate identity, while others seek the critical vantage point of the outsider. The styles and symbols of graphic design, whether invented by professional consultants or taken off the supermarket shelf, give people and products an identity, making them visible to various audiences.

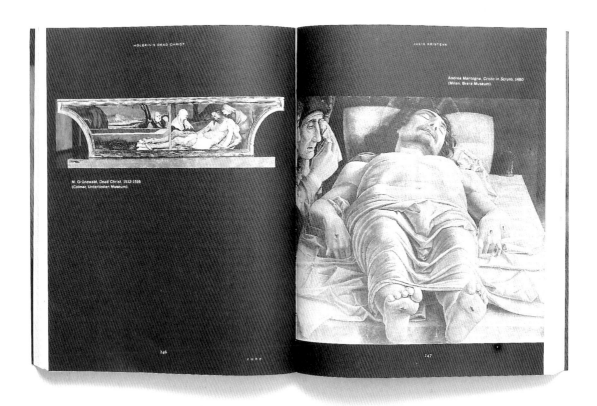

*Zone 3: Fragments for a History
of the Human Body, Part One*
Book, 1989, offset lithograph
Designer: Bruce Mau (b. 1959)
Publisher: Urzone, New York

X-Ray
Magazine, 1994, mixed media (letterpress,
offset, photocopy, collage)
Designer: Johnny Brewton (b. 1966)
Publisher: Pneumatic Press, San Francisco
Collection Cooper-Hewitt, National
Design Museum, Gift of the designer

PUBLISHING

To publish is to make public, to build a community through the exchange of information. From underground periodicals and mass-market fashion magazines to books and electronic media, publishing uses type, pictures, and layout to shape ideas. The covers of books and magazines entice readers to stop and look inside, while electronic "home pages" are seductive points of entry for layers of digital information. The successive leaves of a bound book or the screens of an electronic text employ typography, imagery, and organizational devices to set a dramatic stage for experiencing content. The typographic book, invented in early modern Europe, triggered the birth of international cultures by allowing texts to more easily survive the harrowing journey across geographical and historical boundaries. Springing from the tradition of the handmade manuscript, the printed book quickly developed its own visual conventions. The bulk of typographic history is cradled between the covers of the book, a compact and sturdy container for storing and shipping information. The magazine, a periodically issued "warehouse" of disparate texts, became a mass medium in the nineteenth century. Its mix of typography, illustration, and advertising upset the preeminence of the book as the canonical source of typographic standards. The book and magazine as static, paper-based objects have been challenged by the rise of electronic publishing. CD-ROMs and the Internet have automated our access to data, stimulating the rise of new subcultures linked by information networks. Although the imminent death of the printed page is often predicted by prophets of digital cataclysm, books and periodicals have proven themselves, during the final hours of the twentieth century, to be flexible forms responsive to cultural and technological change. While producers of mass media still dominate the marketplace, the past fifteen years have seen numerous smaller publishers of both print and digital texts address narrower audiences. Short-run books can be customized to meet the needs of specialized readerships, while "fanzines" are informally published newsletters whose production often mixes high technology with crude handicraft. The traditional roles of author, editor, and designer are merging into a new figure, a medieval scribe recast for the twenty-first century.

THE LOVER

MARGUERITE DURAS

The Lover
Book cover, 1983, offset lithograph
Designer and art director:
Louise Fili (b. 1951)
Publisher: Pantheon, New York
Collection Cooper-Hewitt, National
Design Museum, Gift of Steven Heller

One, No
One & One
Hundred
Thousand
Luigi
Pirandello

TRANSLATED BY WILLIAM WEAVER

The
TRANSLATED BY
Baphomet
SOPHIE HAWKES AND
Pierre
STEPHEN SARTARELLI
Klossowski
FOREWORD BY MICHEL FOUCAULT

THE
SONNETS
TO
ORPHEUS
RAINER
MARIA
RILKE
TRANSLATED BY
STEPHEN MITCHELL

The Queen's Throat
· OPERA ·
Homo
SEXUALITY
and the
MYSTERY
of
· DESIRE ·
· WAYNE ·
KOESTENBAUM

The Sonnets to Orpheus
Book cover, 1985, offset lithograph
Designer: Carin Goldberg (b. 1953)
Art director: Frank Metz
Publisher: Simon and Schuster, New York
Collection Cooper-Hewitt, National
Design Museum, Gift of the designer

The Queen's Throat
Book cover, 1993, offset lithograph
Designer: Carin Goldberg
Art director: Frank Metz
Publisher: Simon and Schuster, New York
Collection Cooper-Hewitt, National
Design Museum, Gift of the designer

*Marsilio Fiction Series: One, No One &
One Hundred Thousand* and
The Baphomet
Book covers, 1992, offset lithographs
Designer and art director: Louise Fili
Publisher: Eridanos Press,
Hygiene, Colorado
Collection Cooper-Hewitt, National
Design Museum, Gift of Steven Heller

PUBLISHING

THE **BOOK**

INSIDE AND OUT

A book is often judged by its cover, a tiny poster designed
for up-close viewing. Metaphor and suggestion as well as
large-scale, hard-sell graphics can be used on the front of a
book to compel readers to pick it up and buy it. A contemporary bookshop is a commercial gallery of poster design
writ small, from the rote to the revolutionary.

The dust jacket wrapped around a hardcover book
initially was conceived as a plain protective package to be
thrown away after purchase. The paperback, launched as a
popular medium in the mid-nineteenth century, used woodcut
illustrations to mobilize its cover as a sales tool.[1] Familiar
styles of illustration and typography can identify a book's
genre and intended audience, from calligraphic pink-and-
purple romances for women to spiky black-and-red thrillers
for men. Publishers with higher literary ambitions have
sometimes invited designers to create experimental covers
and jackets, as seen in the work that Alvin Lustig produced in
the 1940s and 1950s for New Directions Books in New York.

Louise Fili opened up the conventions of cover design
when she served as art director for Pantheon Books during
the 1980s. Evolving out of the New York tradition of popular
eclecticism, her covers have drawn liberally on the history of
design, from Art Nouveau to Italian Deco. Fili, who worked
with Herb Lubalin in the 1970s, incorporated his neo-Victorian
pluralism into her own more subtle style. Her gentle palette,

Book Jackets by Alvin Lustig
Booklet, 1947, offset lithograph
Designer: Alvin Lustig (1915-1955)
Publisher: New Directions Books, New York
Collection Cooper-Hewitt, National Design
Museum, Gift of Tamar Cohen

1. On the history of the book, see Lucien
Febvre and Henri-Jean Martin, *The Coming of
the Book: The Impact of Printing 1450-1800*,
trans. David Gerard (London: Verso, 1958);
Warren Chappell, *A Short History of the
Printed Word* (Boston: David R. Godine, 1970);
and Thomas L. Bonn, *An Illustrated History of
American Mass Market Paperbacks* (New York:
Penguin, 1982). See also Piet Schreuders,
*Paperbacks, U.S.A.: A Graphic History,
1939-1959* (San Diego: Blue Dolphin
Enterprises, 1981).

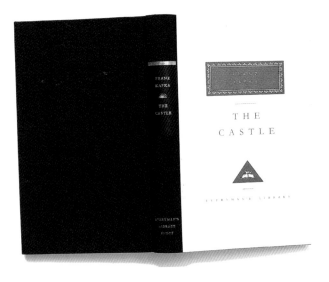

The Castle
Book, 1992, offset lithograph
Designers: Barbara de Wilde (b. 1962)
and Carol Devine Carson (b. 1944)
Publisher: Alfred A. Knopf, New York

Biography
Book jacket, 1991, offset lithograph
Designer: Barbara de Wilde
Art director: Carol Devine Carson
Publisher: Alfred A. Knopf, New York
Collection Cooper-Hewitt, National
Design Museum, Gift of Steven Heller

The History of Luminous Motion
Book, 1989, offset lithograph
Designer: Barbara de Wilde
Publisher: Alfred A. Knopf, New York

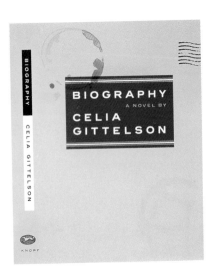

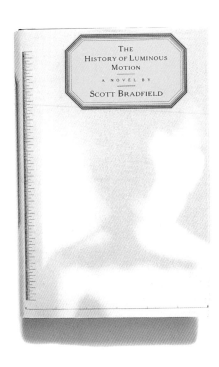

City of Boys
Book jacket, 1991, offset lithograph
Designer: Chip Kidd (b. 1964)
Publisher: Alfred A. Knopf, New York

The American Replacement of Nature
Book jacket, 1991, offset lithograph
Designers: Chip Kidd and Barbara de Wilde
Art director: Peter R. Kruzan
Publisher: Currency/Doubleday, New York
Collection Cooper-Hewitt, National Design
Museum, Gift of Steven Heller

The Lost Father
Book jacket, 1992, offset lithograph
Designer: Barbara de Wilde
Art director: Carol Devine Carson
Publisher: Alfred A. Knopf, New York
Collection Cooper-Hewitt, National Design
Museum, Gift of Steven Heller

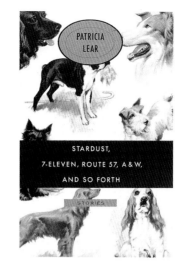

Stardust, 7-Eleven, Route 57, A & W, and So Forth
Book jacket, 1992, offset lithograph
Designer and art director:
Carol Devine Carson
Publisher: Alfred A. Knopf, New York
Collection Cooper-Hewitt, National
Design Museum, Gift of Steven Heller

PUBLISHING

use of historical references, and rejection of glossy finishes in favor of matte laminates reflected the decorative yet restrained post-modernism of the 1980s, made famous by architect Michael Graves. A related body of work was produced by Carin Goldberg, who had worked with Paula Scher at CBS Records in the late 70s before becoming an independent designer for publishers and other clients in New York.[2] The deliberate quietness of Fili's and Goldberg's covers attracted attention on crowded book displays, where the dominant style favored closely packed letterforms aggressively bulging off covers and jackets.

The new tone of voice created by Fili and Goldberg was radically reinflected in the late 1980s by designers at Alfred A. Knopf, a division of Random House. As art director of the Knopf imprint since 1987, Carol Devine Carson has led a team of young designers who have played with elements of the weird, the ugly, and the perverse. Under Carson's direction, Chip Kidd, Archie Ferguson, Barbara de Wilde, and others have transformed bookstore shelves across the country. Jackets incorporating layers of transparent materials have approached the casebound book as a concrete, physical artifact, not simply as a neutral solid to be cheerfully concealed by a paper wrapper. Coffee stains and strands of hair celebrate the book as an intimate object of use, while jackets combining sinister fragments of found images have yielded a literary approach to design where pictures become poetic phrases.[3]

While the covers of books are often bold and sensational, interiors are routinely predictable. In the 1970s and 1980s, Massimo Vignelli helped rethink the book as a total object by

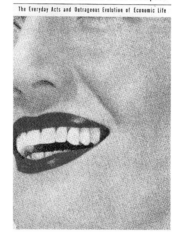

119

2. Philip B. Meggs, "The Women Who Saved New York!" *Print* 43, 1 (January/February 1989): 61-71.
3. See Chip Kidd, "Run with the Dwarves and Win: Adventures in the Book Trade," *Print* 49, 3 (May/June 1995): 21-27. On Carol Devine Carson, see Laurie Haycock Makela and Ellen Lupton, "Underground Matriarchy," *Eye* 14, 4 (autumn 1994): 42-47.

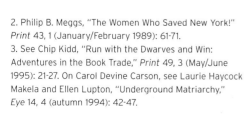

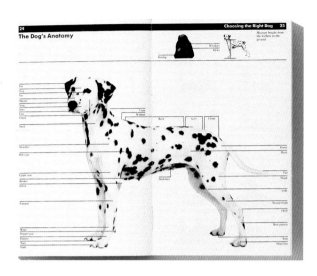

unifying the inside and the outside, the facade and the interior, with an architectural sense of structure. Vignelli conceives of each book as a cinematic sequence in which the placement of images and text refers to a consistent grid. The opening spreads of his books often function like the title sequence of a film—they are dramatically timed preludes to the central action.

Perhaps the most conservative field of book design is academic publishing. Traditionally addressed at narrow audiences trained to ignore the sensual appeal of design, academic books have earned a reputation for dry and dusty graphic presentation. Some presses have respectfully maintained the standards of classical typography, resulting in books of beauty and permanence, while others have gently updated classical structures by turning to such modernist principles as asymmetry and multiple typefaces.[4] Although few academic publishers have pursued an overtly experimental approach, MIT Press is a notable exception. Under the design direction of Muriel Cooper during the 1970s, the press tested new ideas in typography, layout, and production. Today, MIT remains one of the more graphically ambitious university publishers in the United States.

Harper's Illustrated Handbook of Dogs
Book, 1985, offset lithograph
Designer: Massimo Vignelli (b. 1931)
Photographer: John L. Ashbey
Publisher: Harper & Row Publishers, New York
Collection Cooper-Hewitt, National
Design Museum, Gift of the designer

Glas
Book, 1986, offset lithograph
Designer: Richard Eckersley
Publisher: University of Nebraska Press, Lincoln
Collection Cooper-Hewitt, National Design
Museum, Gift of the designer

File Under Architecture
Book, 1974, silkscreen and
offset lithograph
Designer: Muriel Cooper (1925-1994)
Publisher: MIT Press, Cambridge

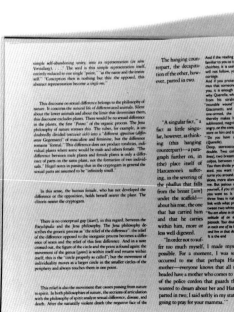

The Telephone Book
Book, 1989, offset lithograph
Designer: Richard Eckersley (b. 1941)
Publisher: University of Nebraska Press, Lincoln
Collection Cooper-Hewitt, National Design
Museum, Gift of the designer

PUBLISHING

Shifts in the literary form of academic writing have encouraged design innovation at the University of Nebraska Press, which has published texts by French philosopher Jacques Derrida, inventor of the term "deconstruction." Designer Richard Eckersley worked with Derrida on the 1986 book *Glas*, written as a collage of literary, philosophical, and scientific fragments. With his design of Avital Ronal's *The Telephone Book* in 1989, Eckersley pushed the visual interpretation of theoretical texts even farther by generating typographic analogues for the author's speculations on electronic media. Eckersley attributes his interpretive license in designing these books to the permissive spirit of the writing as well as the flexibility engendered by desktop page layout systems, which shifted typographic control from the typesetter to the designer.[5]

The transformation of post-structuralism from academic theory into cultural practice is embodied in the publications of Zone Books, founded in 1985 by Jonathan Crary, Hal Foster, Sanford Kwinter, and Michele Feher. The Toronto-based designer Bruce Mau created a visual identity for Zone that jolted the stable norms of academic publishing and contributed significantly to the publisher's success. Lavishing attention on production details, Mau devised gate-folded covers that add formality to Zone's weighty paperback volumes and give readers the pleasure of unfolding a flap to reveal an image concealed inside. Saturated colors transform dull photographs and engravings into dramatic illustrations, while subtly crafted pages of typography impose their own veil of commentary on the texts.

121

4. A useful index of developments in the design of academic books is the publication *AAUP Book, Jacket and Journal Show*, an annual illustrated exhibition catalog (New York: American Association of University Presses).

5. Richard Eckersley, telephone interview with author, August 1994.

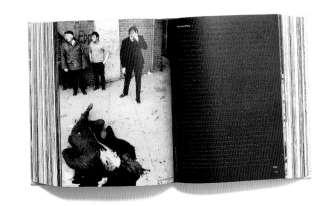

*Zone 4: Fragments for a History
of the Human Body, Part Two*
Book, 1989, offset lithograph
Designer: Bruce Mau (b. 1959)
Publisher: Urzone, New York

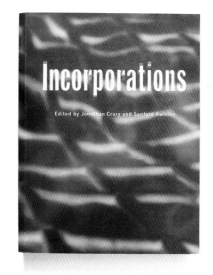

S,M,L,XL
Book, 1995, offset lithograph
Designer: Bruce Mau
with Kevin Sugden, Nigel Smith,
Greg Van Alstyne, Alison Hahn,
and Chris Rowat
Firm: Bruce Mau Design Inc.
Photographer: Hans Werlemann
Publisher: The Monacelli Press, New York

Money The original digital clock.

Abortion Do-it-yourself genocide.

Science fiction The body's dream of becoming a machine.

Answering machines They are patiently training us to think in a language they have yet to invent.

Genetics Nature's linguistic system.

Food Our delight in food is rooted in our immense relish at the thought that, prospectively, we are eating ourselves.

Neurobiology Science's Sistine Chapel.

Criminal science The anatomizing of illicit desire, more exciting than desire itself.

Camouflage The camouflaged battleship or bunker must never efface itself completely, but confuse our recognition systems by one moment being itself, and the next not itself. Many impersonators and politicians exploit the same principle.

Cybernetics The totalitarian systems of the future will be docile and subservient, like super-efficient servants, and all the more threatening for that.

Disease control A proliferation of imaginary diseases may soon be expected, satisfying our need for a corrupt version of ourselves.

Ergonomics The Protestant work ethic disguised as a kinaesthetic language.

Personal computers Perhaps unwisely, the brain is subcontracting many of its core functions, creating a series of branch economies that may one day amalgamate and mount a management buy-out.

277

Zone 6: Incorporations
Book, 1992, offset lithograph
Designer: Bruce Mau
Publisher: Urzone, New York

Mau's design strategies encouraged Zone's editors to publish texts composed in non-academic formats, from timelines and interviews to compilations of deranged dictionary entries. Zone's subject matter traverses such fields as art history, anthropology, literary theory, and psycho-analysis. Working outside the protective umbrella of a university, the editors established Zone as an independent, not-for-profit publishing venture. Zone's image-conscious, interdisciplinary approach reflected the ambitions of a generation of academics who no longer wished to be the guardians of staid and stolid volumes but active, entre-preneurial participants in contemporary life.[6]

Following Zone's lead, The Getty Center for the History of Art and the Humanities, in Santa Monica, became a patron of innovative design in the early 1990s, when editor Julia Bloomfield commissioned book designs from Mau and other designers, including Lorraine Wild and Laurie Haycock Makela. Over the past decade, Wild's book designs for the Whitney Museum of American Art and Haycock Makela's work for the Walker Art Center have helped transform the rigid genre of the exhibition catalog into a medium for interpretive typo-graphy and layout. In a period when artists have challenged the neutrality of reproduction and display, exhibition catalogs have become more than just elegant portfolios of essays and pictures. As the minds of curators and editors open up to the critical potential of graphic design, books are serving not only to represent works of art according to standards of fidelity, but to actively translate complex installations and hybrid objects into the medium of publishing.

124

6. Meighan Gale, managing editor of Zone Books, telephone interview with Ellen Lupton, August 1994. On Bruce Mau, see Will Novosedlik, "The Producer as Author," Eye 15, 4 (winter 1994): 44-53. See also Adele Freedman, "Exploring the No Man's Land Between Art and Design," Toronto Globe and Mail, August 8, 1987; and H. J. Kirchhoff, "Publisher Aims at the Intellect," ibid., April 13, 1988.

Ordonnance For The Five Kinds of Columns After the Method of the Ancients
Book, 1993, offset lithograph
Designer: Lorraine Wild (b. 1953)
Series design: Laurie Haycock Makela and Lorraine Wild
Publisher: Getty Center for the History of Art and the Humanities, Santa Monica
Collection Cooper-Hewitt, National Design Museum, Gift of the designer

Dan Friedman challenged the documentary intentions of exhibition catalogs by mixing photographs of art with seductive media images in his books *Cultural Geometry* (1988), *Artificial Nature* (1990), and *Post-Human* (1992), a series created with curator Jeffrey Deitch for the Deste Foundation for Contemporary Art in Athens, Greece. Friedman used commercial stock photographs taken from the realms of science, journalism, and advertising as cultural counterpoints for issues explored by artists.

Over the past decade, digital technologies have radically altered the way books are produced, placing sensitive typographic tools in the hands of authors, editors, and designers. Since the Renaissance, the physical production of a book has demanded a signficant outlay of capital. A book becomes inexpensive only when large numbers can be sold, diminishing the cost per unit, yet production in significant quantities requires even more capital. New technologies are generating new economies of scale. Such processes as the Xerox Docutech system can print an entire book directly from an electronic file, eliminating the costly manufacture of printing plates and operation of mechanical presses.

Docutech, which can be financially viable for editions ranging from one to one thousand, reflects the book's transformation from a closed, monumental tome to an object that can be customized for specific audiences. Publishing on demand may soon replace publishing on speculation, transforming the reader from a consumer of finished goods into a producer whose needs and desires trigger manufacture.

Artificial Nature
Book, 1990, offset lithograph
Designer: Dan Friedman (1946–1995)
Publisher: Deste Foundation for
Contemporary Art, Athens, Greece
Collection Cooper-Hewitt, National Design
Museum, Gift of the Estate of Dan Friedman

An entirely new spectrum of prints, came down spring's runways, spurred on by designers' fascination with the psychedelic era. Brilliant patchwork. Plaids within plaids. Color-splashed tie-dye. And, of course, stripes and florals were out in force—but reworked in modern shades and sizes. The big news: the use of light, transparent fabrics in layers that all mix and move together, all defining a soft new sexiness for the nineties. Photographed by Patrick Demarchelier

Harper's Bazaar (An Entirely New Spectrum)
Magazine, 1993, offset lithograph
Creative director: Fabien Baron (b. 1959)
Photographer: Patrick Demarchelier

Harper's Bazaar (Slick Skins)
Magazine, 1995, offset lithograph
Creative director: Fabien Baron
Photographer: Raymond Meier

Harper's Bazaar (Boots)
Magazine, 1993, offset lithograph
Creative director: Fabien Baron
Photographer: Raymond Meier

Publisher: The Hearst Corporation, New York

THE **MAGAZINE**

AND BEYOND

While the text of a classical book is a steady stream of words mastered by a single author, the content of a magazine is produced by editors, designers, and advertisers as well as numerous writers working independently from each other. The magazine is a commercial precedent for the postmodern text: literary critics have heralded such features as fragmentation, equivocality, spurious visual effects, and the free mixture of high and low cultural references as hallmarks of a new voice in literature that rejects the formal autonomy of the traditional work of art. The magazine genre has always incorporated the principle of mixed speech.

Magazines were being published in the United States by the 1740s; they became a popular medium in the nineteenth century, when they featured woodcut and lithographic illustrations as well as articles, advertisements, and serialized fiction. The invention, in the 1880s, of the halftone process for reproducing photographs stimulated the birth of the modern magazine. The genre reached maturity in the twentieth century with picture-driven periodicals like *Vogue*, *Harper's Bazaar*, and *Life*. Alexey Brodovitch, art director at *Bazaar* from 1934 to 1958, combined expressive typography with full-bleed images created by vanguard photographers.[7]

Bazaar returned to the forefront of magazine design in 1992 when it was redesigned by Fabien Baron, a French-born graphic designer who had startled the fashion world with his

Harper's Bazaar
Magazine, 1992, offset lithograph
Creative director: Fabien Baron
Photographer: Patrick Demarchelier
Publisher: The Hearst Corporation, New York

7. On twentieth-century magazines, see William Owen, *Modern Magazine Design* (New York: Rizzoli, 1991). For a broader history, see Frank Luther Mott, *A History of American Magazines* (Cambridge: Belknap Press of Harvard University Press, 1967).

Rolling Stone (Alanis Morissette)
Magazine, 1995, offset lithograph
Art director: Fred Woodward (b. 1949)
Designer: Geraldine Hessler
Photographer: Frank Ockenfels 3

Rolling Stone (Martin Scorsese)
Magazine, 1990, offset lithograph
Designer and art director: Fred Woodward
Photographer: Albert Watson

Rolling Stone (Alicia Silverstone)
Magazine, 1995, offset lithograph
Art director: Fred Woodward
Designer: Geraldine Hessler
Photographer: Peggy Sirota

Publisher: Wenner Media, New York

design of Italian *Vogue* in the 1980s. Baron's *Bazaar,* created with editor Elizabeth Tilberis, heralded a "return to elegance." In their opening issue, Baron and Tilberis introduced spectacular feature spreads into the magazine's dense crush of advertising pages, confronting the reader with astonishing feats of typographic formalism and stark photographic imagery. The new *Bazaar* was at once replete with invention and informed by its own history.[8]

Another magazine that reinvented itself during the past decade by reclaiming its heritage was *Rolling Stone.* The magazine's original format, designed by Robert Kingsbury in the late 1960s, gave a decorative spin to the chaotic look of the underground press. By borrowing decorative devices from nineteenth-century typography, such as "scotch rules," borders that combine a thick and a thin line, *Rolling Stone* recalled the flamboyantly off-center dress of *fin de siècle* bohemian dandies. (Victorian bohemia fueled several icons of 1960s counterculture, from the Art Nouveau-inspired psychedelia of Victor Moscoso to the cover of the Beatles' album *Sgt. Pepper's Lonely Hearts Club Band.*) *Rolling Stone* was shaped by a series of art directors, including Mike Salisbury, Roger Black, and Fred Woodward.[9]

When Woodward arrived at the magazine in 1987, *Rolling Stone* had shed its garb of hippy historicism in favor of a tidy format that consistently used the sans serif typeface Franklin Gothic. One of Woodward's first moves was to bring back the decorative border used in the early years of the magazine.[10] The border became the identifying feature of the editorial pages, allowing Woodward to discard Franklin Gothic in favor

Rolling Stone
Magazine, 1993, offset lithograph
Designer and art director: Fred Woodward
Photographer: Andrew MacPherson
Photo editor: Laurie Kratochvil
Publisher: Wenner Media, New York

8. See Fabien Baron, interview with J. Abbott Miller, *Eye* 5, 18 (autumn 1995): 10-16; and Michael Rock, "Fabien Baron, or Sex and a Singular Art Director," *I.D.* (May/June 1993): 44-51.

9. On *Rolling Stone,* see Steven Heller, "The Underground Revisited," *Print* 39 (March/April 1985): 35-43.
10. Fred Woodward, interview with Ellen Lupton, New York, June 1996.

Spy
Magazine, 1987, offset lithograph
Art director: Alexander Isley (b. 1961)
Publisher: Spy Publishing Partners, New York
Collection Cooper-Hewitt, National Design
Museum, Gift of the designer

PUBLISHING

of an unlimited palette of typefaces, many of them created exclusively for the magazine by type designer Jonathan Hoefler. According to Woodward, "Anything that went inside the border was *Rolling Stone*. It was actually very liberating. I was nervous about doing it, afraid that the border would be too confining, but I found that I could try anything within the limits of the border."

Spy took the entire genre of the magazine as a point of departure and an object of relentless parody. *Spy*, published beginning in 1986 and resurrected after a short hiatus in 1994, offers cruel and clever commentaries on the spectacle of New York's high society. Design has always been part of *Spy*'s abrasive personality. The original format was created by Drenttel Doyle Partners, who used the standard anatomy of magazine design to create platforms for editorial play. Founding editor Kurt Andersen had mastered information graphics at *Time* magazine, which in the 1970s had pioneered the use of graphs and charts to make serious information understandable to a broad public. In contrast, *Spy* developed an intentionally arcane look for its off-color information, yielding graphics that ignored the conventional wisdom on legibility and yet were irresistible to read. Stephen Doyle's format reflected his sense of the magazine as a literary form—the pictures in *Spy* often amplify the text, rather than serving as artful illustrations respectfully distanced from content. Doyle recalled, "We let the magazine use its own body parts to point to itself."[11]

The Duchess of Windsor was wrong. Even when her weight dropped to 87 pounds, resulting in hemorrhaging ulcers, she clung with bony hands to a pillow bearing her famous motto. Some call this class. We call it extremism. As NELL SCOVELL discovered, the evidence suggests that indeed, you can be

too rich

& *too thin*

Spy (Too Rich & Two Thin)
Magazine, 1987, offset lithograph
Art director: Alexander Isley
Publisher: Spy Publishing Partners, New York
Collection Cooper-Hewitt, National Design
Museum, Gift of the designer

Art director Alexander Isley perfected *Spy*'s distinctive use of tables, diagrams, and flow charts, creating a rich and witty editorial form widely imitated in other publications, from *Entertainment Weekly* to the *New York Times*. A device indebted to *Spy* is to treat images as if they are type by injecting icons and tiny photographs into the body of the copy. Since the late 1980s, an obsession with the typographic materiality of the printed page—more styles and sizes of type, more dropped caps and pullout quotes, more heads and subheads—has indicated a renewed *writerliness* in magazine design. Design consultant Roger Black commented in 1990, "Art directors used to be frustrated illustrators and photographers. Now they're frustrated writers and editors."[11]

As early as 1959, Herb Lubalin credited television with forcing attention on the relationship between word and image in print advertising. In the 1960s, Marshall McLuhan predicted the rise of a progressively visual culture and the collapse of the "Gutenberg Galaxy." McLuhan's invocation of television as the democratic spirit of the age echoed the technological optimism of the 1920s Constructivist avant-garde. Moholy-Nagy and El Lissitzky were entranced by mechanically mediated pictures—photographic, lithographic, and tele-graphic—as the basis of a universal language. Remarks on the rapid replacement of words with images are common among intellectuals today.[13] Critic Joseph Giovannini mourned the lost literary integrity of magazines in 1989, blaming "competition from television, the VCR, and other nonprint media" for spawning "agressively designed pages that freely mix and cut words, photographs, and graphic devices."[14]

Spy (Naked City)
Magazine, 1988, offset lithograph
Art director: Alexander Isley
Design consultants: Drenttel Doyle Partners
Publisher: Spy Publishing Partners, New York
Collection Cooper-Hewitt, National Design Museum,
Gift of the designer

Spy (Family Ties)
Magazine, 1988, offset lithograph
Art director: Alexander Isley
Publisher: Spy Publishing Partners, New York
Collection Cooper-Hewitt, National Design
Museum, Gift of the designer

131

11. Quoted in Ellen Lupton, "Bye, Spy: An Obit for the '80s," *Print* 43, 3 (May/June 1994): 111-12.
12. Quoted in Ellen Lupton, "Post-Saturday Evening Post: Magazine Design and its Dis-Contents," *Print* 44, 6 (November/December): 58-67.
13. See Neil Postman, *Amusing Ourselves to Death* (New York: Penguin, 1985).
14. Joseph Giovannini, "A Zero Degree of Graphics," in *Graphic Design in America*, ed. Mildred Friedman (Minneapolis: Walker Art Center, 1989): 201-13.

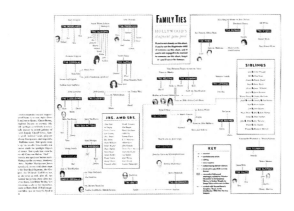

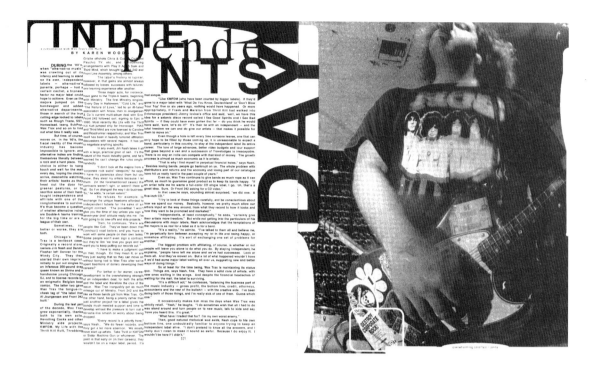

Ray Gun (Independents Day)
Magazine, 1993, offset lithograph
Designer and art director: David Carson
Photographer: David Simms
Publisher: Ray Gun Publishing, Santa Monica
Collection Cooper-Hewitt, National Design
Museum, Gift of Steven Heller

Beach Culture
Magazine, 1990, offset lithograph
Designer and art director: David Carson
Publisher: Surfer Publications, Inc., Los Angeles
Collection Cooper-Hewitt, National Design
Museum, Gift of Steven Heller

Despite the rising tide of images in contemporary culture, however, words continue to proliferate. Even television, the medium so commonly reviled as literacy's executioner, has become increasingly saturated with typography. Pictures have not, in fact, replaced text in contemporary media; instead, words have become more physical, more embodied, more pictorial. Sophisticated illustration was a hallmark of magazines in the 1970s, exemplified by the influential format created for *New York Magazine* by Walter Bernard and Milton Glaser in 1968. In the 1980s and 1990s, editorial designers have been fascinated with typography, using marginalia, pullout quotes, information graphics, and other devices to interrupt the unity of the classical linear text.

Typographic pyrotechnics found an explosive outlet in the work of David Carson, whose designs for the California magazines *Beach Culture* and *Ray Gun* have been widely publicized, making Carson one of the few designers to become a pop culture hero. Carson's typography serves not just to present and intepret editorial content, but often takes the place of content—in the traditional verbal sense—altogether. His style, which has its roots in the typographic experiments initiated at Cranbrook and CalArts, provided a visual language for Generation X, a secret code whose messages are embedded not in words but in the peculiar forms and configurations the alphabet itself can take.[15]

Beach Culture and *Ray Gun* visualized the desires and ambitions of specific subcultures. Precedents for such canons of street style include the British magazines *The Face* and *ID*. As art director of *The Face*—and other magazines—during

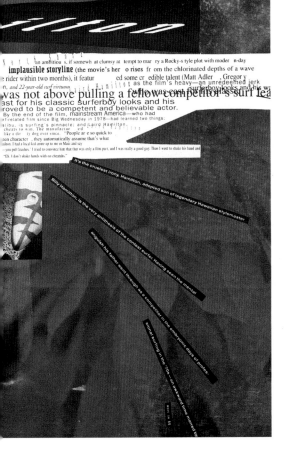

133

15. David Carson and Lewis Blackwell, *The End of Print: The Graphic Design of David Carson* (San Francisco: Chronicle Books, 1995). See also David Carson,"American Typo," interview with Tom Eslinger and Brian Smith, *World Art* 1 (1995): 72-76.

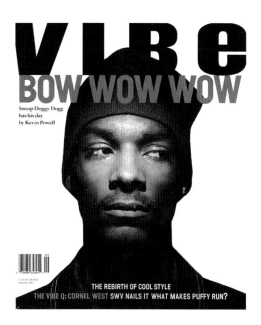

the 1980s, Neville Brody developed a typographic approach that was, in turns, futuristic and atavistic. He generated strange new letterforms while letting old ones—such as Helvetica—flash briefly back into fashion. Brody, like David Carson a few years later, was able to transfer the subcultural cachet of his magazine work to the field of advertising, creating distinctive campaigns for Nike and other manufacturers who sought to appeal to the youth markets addressed by his magazines.[16]

Numerous publications target the interests of particular subcultures. *Urb* was founded in Los Angeles by Raymond Roker, who is the magazine's publisher, editor, and art director. Roker created *Urb* to chronicle the culture of rap and hip-hop. Initially printed on newsprint and given away locally, *Urb* is now produced in four colors and distributed nationwide on newstands. *Vibe*, backed by Time Warner, was introduced in 1993 as a more commercial venture than *Urb* that covers similar territory. *YSB (Young Sisters and Brothers)*, directed at African-American teenagers and young adults, builds an educational message into its treatment of contemporary black music and culture. *Sí*, founded in 1996, is aimed at Hispanic and Latino Americans, while *A.* speaks to what publisher Jeff Yang calls "Generation A"—young Asian Americans. Drawing these magazines together is the desire to represent youthfulness through type and image.[17]

Such bibles of culture and style as *Rolling Stone, Ray Gun,* and *Urb* have enabled subcultures to expand and find wider recognition outside their own ranks: to go public through publishing. Another variant of the contemporary

134

16. Rick Poynor, "Neville Brody Faces the Future," *I.D.* (September/October 1994): 38-47; Jon Wozencroft, *The Graphic Language of Neville Brody* (New York: Rizzoli, 1988).

17. On magazines directed at youth minorities, see Somini Sengupta, "In their Own Image," *New York Times,* April 28, 1996.

Between C and D
Magazine, 1988, offset lithograph
Designer and publisher unknown
New York

Bad Newz 15
Magazine, 1990, offset lithograph
Designer and publisher: Bob Z.,
San Francisco

Sí, logo for magazine, 1996
Design director: Rip Georges (b. 1946)
Publisher: Sí Magazine Limited Partners,
Los Angeles

Urb Magazine
Magazine, 1994, offset lithograph
Designer and art director:
Raymond Leon Roker (b. 1968)
Photographer: Roger Erickson
Publisher: URB Magazine, Los Angeles
Collection Cooper-Hewitt, National
Design Museum, Gift of the designer

Vibe
Magazine, 1993, offset lithograph
Design director: Gary Koepke
Photographer: Dan Winters
Publisher: Time Inc. Ventures, New York

YSB (Young Sisters and Brothers)
Magazine, 1992, offset lithograph
Creative directors: Fo Wilson (b. 1955)
and Elizabeth Rodriguez
Firm: Studio W, Inc.
Publisher: Paige Publications, New York
Collection Cooper-Hewitt, National
Design Museum, Gift of YSB

magazine defines itself by the very narrowness of its reach: the *fanzine*, a sporadically issued periodical that eschews formal systems of distribution in favor of underground networks and word-of-mouth. Fanzines, or zines, often are addressed to intimate circles of friends or to people committed to specific forms of music, film, fashion, literature, or sexuality. The prehistory of the contemporary zine lies in what historians of the genre call "first fandom," the science fiction subculture spawned in the 1920s. The punk music scene of the late 1970s, whose adherents assembled found images and type into raw layouts reproduced on photocopy machines, provides a more direct line to current production. Zine production mushroomed in the 1980s with the advent of desktop publishing systems and the increased range of services offered by photocopy outlets. With an average circulation of 200, most zines are resolutely obscure.[18]

The non-linear structure of the magazine, with its mix of verbal and visual matter, is the printed prototype for multimedia publishing. Also known as "hypermedia" and "new media," multimedia entails the production of documents that combine text, images, video, and animation in a format that is electronically experienced and randomly accessed.[19] This mode of publishing draws on aspects of the traditional book (a coherent body of information packaged in a single volume), the magazine (a diverse collection of disconnected pictures and texts), and television (a medium of electronic spectatorship grounded in the luminous presence of the moving picture). Since the 1950s, television has been alternately condemned as marking the death of literacy and celebrated

18. Michelle Rau, "Towards a History of Fanzine Publishing: From APA to Zines," *Alternative Media* (spring/ summer 1994): 10-13.

19. See George P. Landow, *Hypertext: The Convergence of Contemporary Critical Theory and Technology* (Baltimore: Johns Hopkins University Press, 1992).

Wired
Magazine, September/October 1993,
offset lithograph
Designers: Barbara Tuhr and Tricia McGillis
Publisher: Wired USA Ltd., San Francisco

PUBLISHING

for delivering an enhanced literacy of the eye. Today, the convergence of electronic texts, images, and information technologies is leading to a new form of "book" that combines the electric allure of the video screen with a capacity for storing and accessing data that far exceeds that of conventional print.

The theory of hypermedia was first articulated in 1945 by Vannevar Bush, a computer scientist who proposed a system called "Memex," a desk-sized device for the storage, retrieval, and authoring of information. The Memex unit would employ enhanced versions of technologies that were then current, including microfilm, voice-recognition, keyboard entry, automated data sorting, an array of mechanical buttons and levers, and a system of "dry photography." The core of Bush's proposal lay not in these specific technologies—which seem quaint in retrospect—but in the principle of "associative indexing," by which the user of the Memex device could build links between diverse data stored on microfiche within the body of the desk. Bush wrote, "When numerous items have been thus joined together to form a trail, they can be reviewed in turn, rapidly or slowly....It is exactly as though the physical items had been gathered together from widely separated sources and bound together to form a new book."[20] Computer scientist Ted Nelson expanded Bush's theory of the "new book," giving it the name "hypertext" in 1960.

Hypermedia publishing did not become commercially viable until the late 1980s and early 1990s, when the various technologies it requires became available for use on desktop computers. Building on ideas pioneered by computer

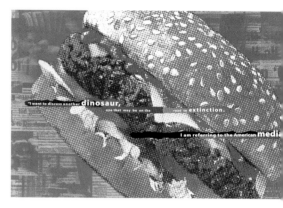

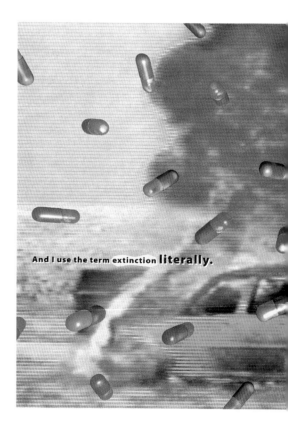

136

20. Vannevar Bush, "As We May Think," *Atlantic Monthly* 176 (July 1945): 101-18.

Blender
CD-ROM, 1995
Editor: Howard Stringer
Creative director: Jason Pearson
Programmer: David Cherry
Publisher: Dennis Publishing, Inc., New York

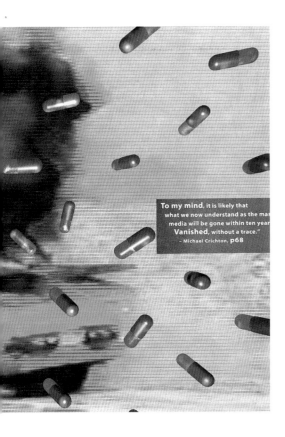

To my mind, it is likely that
what we now understand as the mass
media will be gone within ten years.
Vanished, without a trace."
– Michael Crichton, **p68**

scientists and designers of video games and computer interfaces, several companies began producing hypermedia "publications" on laserdisc and CD-ROM. In the emerging conventions of the electronic document, metaphoric "buttons" and "windows" replaced the mechanical levers and microfilmed pages envisioned by Bush in 1945.

The mixing of ready-made material is central to the production of hypermedia. In the words of designers Bob Cotton and Richard Oliver, "In twenty years' time, one definition of 'literacy' may be the ability to put together an interactive communication (using sound, images, animation and live action video as well as text). If this is the case, it will be largely because hypermedia is the supreme medium for *bricolage*,...the bringing together of existing elements to create something new."[21] The on-line magazine *Blender*, founded in 1995 by Felix Dennis, borrows its evocative title from the domestic countertop to convey the principle of electronic mixing. The promise of hypermedia is, ultimately, to put the disk jockey's turntable into the hands of the dancers on the floor.

The democratic potential of new media is being tested across the circuits of the World Wide Web. This rapidly expanding outgrowth of the Internet, a chain of computers linked around the globe by telephone wires, has allowed a communications system formerly controlled by governments and universities to be accessed by a broader public. That public has used the Web to fulfill a mix of agendas, from the Net's traditional function of providing e-mail communication and access to information, to such new activities as adver-

137

21. Bob Cotton and Richard Oliver, *Understanding Hypermedia: From Multimedia to Virtual Reality* (London: Phaidon Press, 1993).

Consumer Product
CD-ROM, 1994
Art director: Bill Barminski
Technical director: Jerry Hesketh
Producer/director: Webster Lewin
Publisher: Consumer Productions, Los Angeles

Dazzeloids
CD-ROM, 1994
Director and graphics: Rodney A. Greenblatt
Animation and design: Jenny Horn and Trish Booten
Publisher: Voyager, New York

tising, shopping, and commercial publishing. These expanded functions have stimulated the demand to see and display compelling images, strong corporate identities, and accessible user interfaces. Restrictions regarding typography, layout, and the size of image files on the Web are rapidly diminishing, allowing designers greater visual freedom.[22]

The Web hosts a range of discourses, from electronic fanzines to elaborately produced product promotions. Advertisers eager to assert their presence on the Web find themselves in the curious postion of providing not only vivid sales pitches but also content—from corporate time lines to on-line soap operas—interesting enough to engage browsers for extended periods. Designers have a role to play not only in glamorizing commercial messages but in shaping meaningful content on the Web.[23]

If CD-ROMs are electronic analogues to the book— finished documents delivered to consumers in tidy packages—publishing on the Web has closer ties to the magazine, a genre whose character and content must be sustained across time, never located in any single issue. The vitality of a Web site depends on continual revision, dying out when authorship reaches a halt. The Web is an ephemeral medium whose audience seeks constant change.

Visionary explorations of on-screen typography are being conducted at the Visual Language Workshop (VLW) of MIT's Media Lab. The VLW has aimed to build a language that will enable future designers to make complex, malleable documents in real time and three-dimensional space. The goal is to make relationships such as size, brightness, color,

138

22. Jessica Helfand, "A Flock of Ducks: Design and the New Webbed Utopia," *Six Essays on Design and New Media* (New York: William Drenttel, 1995). See also Dave Tubbs, "Pop, Fizz, and Dance," *Internet World* (November 1995): 73-79.

23. On the poverty of content on the Web, see Daniel Drennan, "Smoke and Mirrors on the World Wide Web," *AIGA Journal of Graphic Design* 13, 2 (1995): 17.

24. Muriel Cooper, interview with author, Cambridge, May 1994.

transparency, and location in depth shift in response to the user's position in a document. These cues would enable readers and writers of interactive media to navigate intuitively through levels of information. Shortly before her death in 1994, director Muriel Cooper described the terrain she was exploring: "In the new electronic medium, all sorts of things are up for grabs—authorship, how people read, how people gather and generate material for their own purposes."[24]

Graphic design is central to the publishing process, serving not only to promote the exterior identity of books and magazines but to shape their internal content. New technologies have altered the production of conventional documents, giving graphic designers greater control over the structure of the printed page. Digital layout tools and inexpensive reproduction methods have brought small-scale publishing within the reach of independent producers, who often combine the roles of designer, editor, writer, and distributor. The death of the book, whose murder by television has been predicted since the 1950s, no longer seems imminent. Its supremacy as our culture's most prestigious container for knowledge, however, is already being challenged. As never before, graphic designers have the opportunity to give meaning to new forms of media that are arising from the collision and convergence of old genres and changing technologies.

Shift Online
Home page, 1994, World Wide Web
Designer: Jessica Helfand (b. 1960)
Producer: Dan Pelson
Editor: Jonathan Van Meter
Publisher: Icon International, New York

139

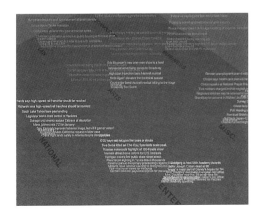

Digital Landscape
Computer interface, 1994
Designer: Yin Yin Wong
Publisher: Visible Language Workshop,
MIT Media Laboratory, Cambridge

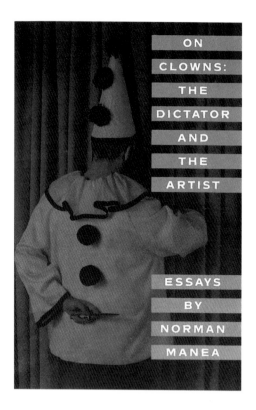

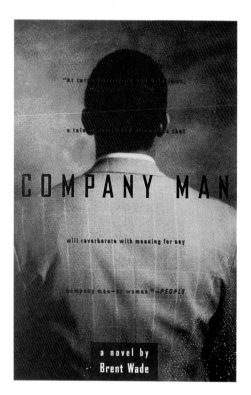

On Clowns: The Dictator and the Artist
Book jacket, 1992, offset lithograph
Designer and art director:
Krystyna Skalski (b. 1952)
Photographer: Geof Kern
Publisher: Grove Weidenfeld, New York
Collection Cooper-Hewitt, National Design
Museum, Gift of Steven Heller

Cardinal Numbers
Book cover, 1988, offset lithograph
Designer: Marc J. Cohen
Art director: Sarah Eisenman
Publisher: Alfred A. Knopf, New York
Collection Cooper-Hewitt, National Design
Museum, Gift of Steven Heller

Company Man
Book cover, 1992, offset lithograph
Designer: iT Design
Art director: Julie Duquet
Photographer: Barry Marcus
Publisher: Doubleday/Anchor Books, New York
Collection Cooper-Hewitt, National Design
Museum, Gift of Steven Heller

Free Agents
Book jacket, c. 1984, offset lithograph
Designer: Steven Guarnaccia (b. 1953)
Art director: Joseph Montebello
Publisher: Harper & Row, New York
Collection Cooper-Hewitt, National Design
Museum, Gift of Steven Heller

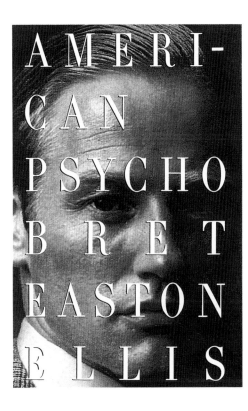

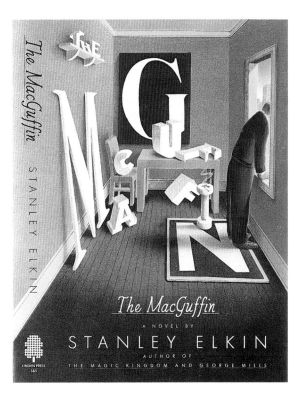

American Psycho
Book cover, 1991, offset lithograph
Designer: Lloyd Ziff
Art director: Susan Mitchell
Photographer: Robert Erdmann
Publisher: Vintage Books, New York
Collection Cooper-Hewitt, National Design
Museum, Gift of Steven Heller

The MacGuffin
Book jacket, 1991, offset lithograph
Designer: Fred Marcellino (b. 1939)
Publisher: Simon & Schuster, New York
Collection Cooper-Hewitt, National Design
Museum, Gift of Steven Heller

The American Way of Birth
Book cover, 1992, offset lithograph
Designer and art director: Neil Stuart
Publisher: Dutton/Penguin Books, New York
Collection Cooper-Hewitt, National Design
Museum, Gift of Steven Heller

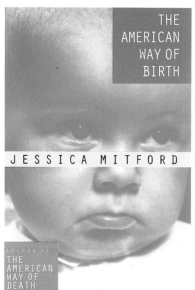

Sylvia
Book cover, 1992, offset lithograph
Designer and art director:
Steven Brower (b. 1952)
Publisher: Carol Publishing Group, New York
Collection Cooper-Hewitt, National Design
Museum, Gift of Steven Heller

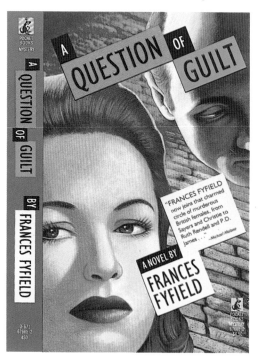

A Question of Guilt
Book cover, 1991, offset lithograph
Designer: Paul Davis (b. 1939)
Art director: Barbara Buck
Publisher: Pocket Books, New York
Collection Cooper-Hewitt, National Design
Museum, Gift of Steven Heller

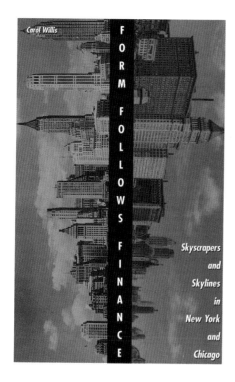

Form Follows Finance
Book cover, 1995, offset lithograph
Designer: Allison Saltzman (b. 1970)
Publisher: Princeton Architectural
Press, New York

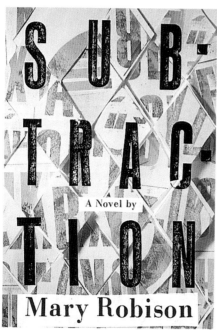

Subtraction
Book jacket, 1995, offset lithograph
Designer: Benita Raphan (b. 1962)
Art director: Carol Devine Carson (b. 1944)
Publisher: Alfred A. Knopf, New York
Collection Cooper-Hewitt, National Design
Museum, Gift of the designer

Life Force
Book jacket, 1991, offset lithograph
Designer: Michael Ian Kaye (b. 1964)
and Melissa Hayden (b. 1951)
Photography: Art Resource
Publisher: Viking Penguin, New York
Collection Cooper-Hewitt, National
Design Museum, Gift of Steven Heller

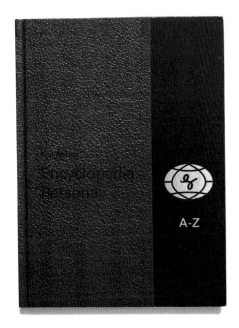

Encyclopedia Persona
Exhibition catalog, 1993, offset lithograph
Designer: Susan Silton (b. 1956)
Concept: Kim Abeles, Karen Moss,
and Susan Silton
Publisher: Fellows of Contemporary Art and
Santa Monica Museum of Art, Los Angeles
Collection Cooper-Hewitt, National Design
Museum, Gift of the designer

THE IMAGE OF ST. BERNADETTE

IMAGE OF ST. BERNADETTE, THE (1987). In 1858, at the age of fourteen, Bernadette Soubirous (1844–1879) saw the Virgin Mary. Bernadette, the daughter of an unemployed miller and an overworked mother, lived in a condemned jailhouse.

Bernadette Soubirous at age fourteen, the year she saw the Virgin Mary

The city officials of Lourdes refused to house prisoners in those conditions. She was a beautiful girl, described as "womanly" by Franz Werfel in his book *The Song of Bernadette*.

On the chilly morning of February 11, Bernadette and her friends went to look in the woods for bones to sell to the rag-and-bone man. She wandered away from the others and came upon a cave-like recess where she sat down to take off her wet socks. There she saw the Virgin Mary, or the "lady" as Bernadette referred to her. The girl thought this Lady to be more elegant than any earthly possibility. "When you have seen her once, you just long to die so that you can see her again."

The Basilica that stands over the grotto where four million visitors each year continue to drink and bathe in the holy waters looking for cures to illnesses and misfortunes.

Lourdes, France. Site of the visions and holy grotto.
ENCYCLOPEDIA PERSONA drawing

Willing Suspension of Disbelief. 1987. Acrylic on canvas replicating patterns on St. Bernadette's clothing, photograph of St. Bernadette, acrylic on canvas rose, metal, wood, bicycle wheel, 68" x 54-1/2" x 22". Collection of Museum of Contemporary Art, Los Angeles, CA.
Daniel Martinez

Souvenir

56

THE IMAGE OF ST. BERNADETTE

Souvenir Dispensary. 1987. Souvenir holy cards of St. Bernadette, altered cosmetic dispenser, photographs of Abeles' painting of St. Bernadette bold, locks of hair, currency, enamel, 21-1/2" x 12" x 13". Collection of Greg and Kristen Escalante, Naples, CA.

Daniel Martinez

Children! Sit Still! 1987. Acrylic painting of St. Bernadette on photo-sensitized fabric, enamel, metal, altered piano stool, violin rests, mirror at base that correctly shows the signature of St. Bernadette (her name is written backwards underneath the stool), lace, satin, 44" x 18-1/2" x 18-1/2".
Daniel Martinez

Souvenir. 1987. Hair, silkscreen and offset print on cardstock, 4-3/4" x 3". Edition of 900. Abeles placed the souvenir holy cards in telephone booths at Lourdes in 1987.

57

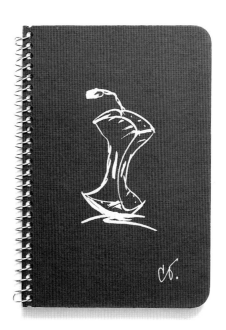

Claes Oldenburg
Exhibition catalog, 1993, offset
lithograph
Designers: John Coy (b. 1943),
Laurie Handler (b. 1955), and
Janine Vigus (b. 1953)
Art director: John Coy
Photographers: Sidney B. Felsen
and Douglas M. Parker
Publisher: Gemini G.E.L., Los Angeles
Collection Cooper-Hewitt, National
Design Museum, Gift of John Coy

To create these exhibition catalogs, the
designers used materials, layout, scale, and
construction techniques to create a concrete,
physical environment for experiencing the
reproduction and display of art. John Coy's
design for *Claes Oldenburg* is a tiny, wire-
bound sketch book printed on uncoated
paper. Susan Silton's catalog for Kim Abeles
employs leatherette binding, foil stamping,
and distinctive typographic styling to evoke
the feeling of a grade-school encyclopedia.

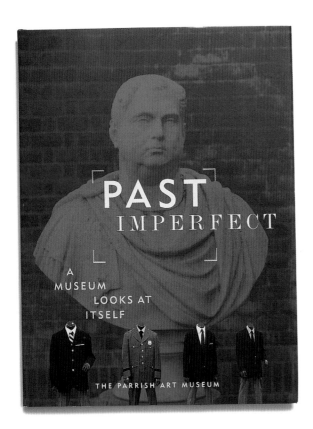

Past Imperfect: A Museum Looks at Itself
Exhibition catalog, 1993, offset lithograph
Designer: Barbara Glauber (b. 1962)
Publisher: The Parrish Art Museum,
Purchase, New York
Collection Cooper-Hewitt, National Design
Museum, Gift of the designer

The Body: Photographs of the Human Form
Book, 1994, offset lithograph with silkscreened
plastic slipcase
Designers: Lucille Tenazas (b. 1953)
and Todd Foreman (b. 1963)
Art director: Lucille Tenazas
Firm: Tenazas Design
Photographer: Tono Stano
Publisher: Chronicle Books, San Francisco
Collection Cooper-Hewitt, National Design
Museum, Gift of the designer

*Problems and Solutions: Surveying the
Work of Jon Tower*
Exhibition catalog, 1992, offset lithograph
Designer: Laura Lacy-Sholly (b. 1965)
and James Sholly (b. 1965)
Firm: Antenna
Publisher: Herron Gallery, Indianapolis Center
for Contemporary Art
Collection Cooper-Hewitt, National Design
Museum, Gift of the designers

Strange Attractors
Book, 1989, offset lithograph
Designers: Tibor Kalman (b. 1949)
and Marlene McCarty (b. 1957)
Firm: M&Co.
Publisher: The New Museum, New York
Collection Cooper-Hewitt, National Design
Museum, Gift of Tibor Kalman

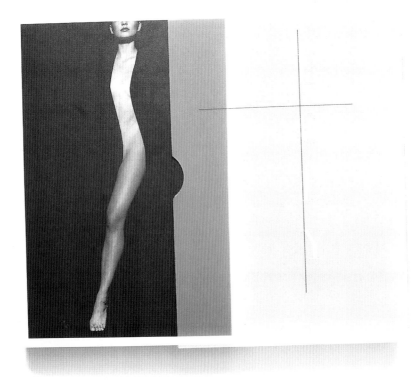

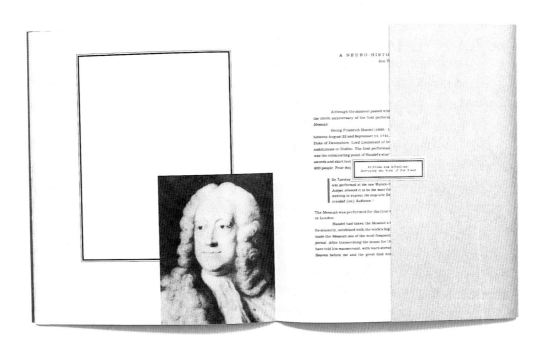

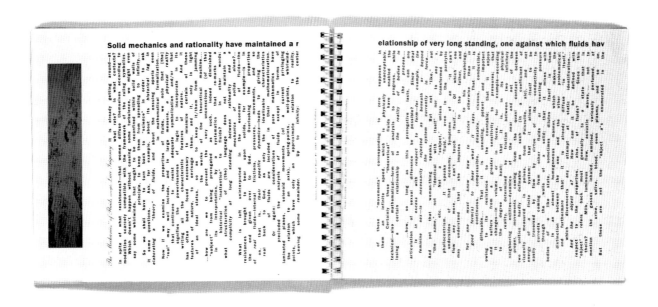

METALWORK 1793–1880

SILVER VESSELS IN
BALTIMORE REPOUSSE STYLE
1830–80

SLAVE SHACKLES
Maker unknown
Made in Baltimore, c. 1793–1872

DOLLHOUSE
Maker unknown, c. 1860s

Mining the Museum
Exhibition catalog, 1994, offset lithograph
Designer: Charles Nix (b. 1967)
Publisher: New Press, New York

To create the exhibition *Mining the Museum*, artist
Fred Wilson took objects from the collection of
the Maryland Historical Society in Baltimore and
displayed them in ways that revealed the
marginalized representation of African Americans.
For example, Wilson aimed a timed spotlight at a
formal portrait and alternated its focus between
the central white "subjects" of the painting and the
black slaves who occupy the edges. Designer
Charles Nix used die cuts and cropping to translate
Wilson's display strategies into the medium of
the book.

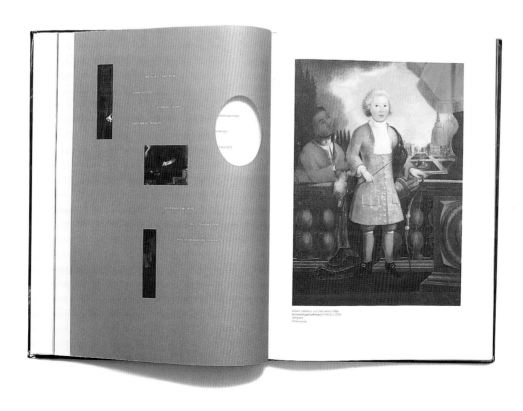

Dislocations
Exhibition catalog, 1991, offset lithograph
Designers: Stephen Doyle (b. 1956)
and Andrew Gray
Creative directors: Stephen Doyle
and William Drenttel (b. 1953)
Firm: Drenttel Doyle Partners
Museum of Modern Art, New York
Collection Cooper-Hewitt, National Design
Museum, Gift of Drenttel Doyle Partners

This exhibition catalog uses classical
typography in an anti-classical way. Large-
scale capitals are scattered arbitrarily
across the opening pages, and headline
typography mixes with body text.

LOUISE BOU
RGEOIS CHRI
S BURDEN SO
PHIE CALLE
DAVID HAMM
ONS ILYA KA
BAKOV BRUC
E NAUMAN A
DRIAN PIPER

PUBLIC
ENEMY

91

ARTIST'S NOTES

I think we're pretty much numb to the visual arts in New York City. But we still have to go out and 55
attempt it, even if you know you're failing. It's like watching basketball. There's no play that hasn't
been made. So in art I'm slightly impressed once in a while, but mainly I'm trying to find a new
vocabulary that I'm not used to, that frightens me and brings richness to me and this great city.
| It's hard dealing with that white cube. I don't see the importance of interacting with it. To me it's
like playing Carnegie Hall or Lincoln Center. I started off showing on paintboards in Jewish recre-
ation centers because they were the only ones in Los Angeles that gave shows to black artists. I've
shown around swimming pools, with art on easels, art on trees, in bars, in barbershops and cafés.
I've done all that. The white walls are so difficult because everything is out of context. They don't
give me any information. It's not the way my culture perceives the world. We would never build a
shape like that or rooms that way. To us that's for mad people, you get put in them in the hospital.

DAVID HAMM
There's no other place that I'd seen that kind of room until I came into the art world. | I'm pre-
ONS
pared, regardless. You have to be prepared to burst in that ray of
light when it comes and do with it whatever. I have to meet the
challenge. It's a good feeling to try and outsmart myself. This challenge is incredible because the
white space is not giving any information back. You have to bring everything to it. | Art is a way
to keep from getting damaged by the outside world, to keep the negative energy away. Otherwise
you absorb it, if you don't have a shield to let it bounce off of. Then you really go crazy. | It's like
listening to Sun Ra's music. It's so beyond blackness, or whiteness. It's over and beyond the rain-
bow. | Cultural statements in art can damage free thought or no-thought, which is the best thought.
I would love to be free enough to have no thoughts. FROM AN INTERVIEW WITH ROBERT STORR

Opposit: David Hammons. Preparatory sketch for PUBLIC ENEMY. 1991. Pencil on paper. 8½ x 11". Photo: Erik Landsberg

The positions of the chapter titles
are dictated by an opening list of
artists' names that have been forced
to occupy a justified block.

THE NEW URBAN LAND SCAPE

TABLE *of* CONTENTS

The city is an aesthetic expectation and plan, but the nature of that plan is also so idiosyncratically and socially determined that art and the city may seem irreconcilable, even while they are metaphors for one another. Richard Martin observes The New Urban Landscape: Spectators in the Visionary

CITY

IF, IN SPENGLER'S ADAGE, the narrative arts presuppose the world-city, the map and landscape of the city are the geography of the visual arts as well. The city that is macrocosm of a world — even an uncharted sphere — and the macrocosm of art — even an inchoate aesthetic — is a metaphor as familiar as a city of God or an emerald city of longing and long dream. The artists of *The New Urban Landscape* enter into the persistent yearning of art indicative of complex urban life. Thus affiliated with art's abiding ambition and with urbanism's constant presence, these artists also reveal the particular character of the city today, an old idea in new forms.

Is the city today — or, at least, our perception of it — fundamentally different from the succession of cities that have previously existed? It may seem a vaunting zeal to pose a new city on the site of its multiple and continuous incarnations. Like modernism and modernity, the city is constantly reinvented in the mind and in its objects. Like modernism and modernity, the city in the 1980s poses the possibility of difference, or new inflection (which is not to argue for a factitious postmodernism that fades into nothing more than a newly inflected modernism), but a city that sustains the urban tradition, yet transfigures it in the specific habits of the 1980s.

Ever has the city been the site, for instance, of rapacious greed and the differentiation of classes determined in substance by money. There have been idyllic times when one sought the democratic city, whether in the idealism of public amenities and common grounds or in the expressed goals of shared values, but our decade has given little to unify the city. Instead, politicians build on their division of social classes, ethnic groups, and diverse interests to consolidate a stratum of power above adverse concerns and demands. Urban

contrast is no longer a matter of crossing from one precinct into another, acknowledging that isolated problems exist, but the visible dialectic that universal problems permeate the opulent urban complex, made manifest in addicts that menace pedestrians wherever they walk, the shattered homeless who have taken the city at large to be what no designated site can be for their forced vagabondage, and the tolerance to such incivilities as trash and dirt that were once thought to be banished from the ivory colossus of the city. Under these circumstances, the traditional concept of grandeur for the city can barely exist. The urban metaphor in the 1980s requires new terms.

Roland Barthes tells us that de Maupassant, realizing that the Eiffel Tower was visible from every part of his city, determined to evade it by dining regularly in the restaurant there, enjoying not the food, but the opportunity to avoid seeing the monument. To be sure, in not seeing, he had become even more physically involved in

the city's structure and in the very monument that he sought to elude. In the 1980s, art neither escapes the city nor does it perceive the city from on high. Rather, art addresses the infrastructure of human systems, technology, the environment, and the humane condition of the urban landscape.

Haim Steinbach's *Adirondack Tableau* may indicate the delicate place and the tough positioning of art of the city. Reversing de Maupassant's stratagem, Steinbach places his work on the bridge across Liberty Street (its name already redolent of urban history and dream) between windows into the urban direction and to the Hudson River. The traditional promise of art invested in nature the paradise of perfect forms only to be replicated by works of art in a naturalistic tradition or emulated by art of abstracting proclivity. Steinbach compels the contradiction and makes no reconciliation. He does not allow for art's easy triumph in tandem with nature, nor does he permit art to assume the autocratic and technological posture of a modern system capable of subduing nature. Rather, Steinbach's wall with aperture is more substantively a barrier than a passage. Discordant with the natural majesty of the Hudson, Steinbach's almost kitschy Adirondack envi-

ronment is the perspective, from one side, of nature transformed into commodity and the self-consciousness of nature made into a convention. From another side, literally and figuratively, the ungrowing cabin-in-bench sward is anomalous with urban elevations beyond taking on the terms of advertising as if it were a billboard for holiday trips placed in an urban complex. What Steinbach has created is not convincing as a natural product, so manifest is its cliché of an urban phenomenon, so indefinite in the scale and decisiveness of urban art expression.

It is, of course, an assertion about art, its title designating not only the vignette of wall and bench, but the French tradition of the grand painting. The wall, in this interpretation, is only a frame to the window as the traditional simile to the painting's eye and becomes insubstantial to the perspectives in two directions. Reduced to frame or focus, the wall becomes our point of perception for city and nature, both in their extreme forms, nature exemplified by the great river and the city by one of the tallest buildings in the world. Two hand-carved owls are the human simulation of a natural form, yet they are patently of the world of the humanly created, not of some taxidermy extending the real.

18

19

The first
request Gulliver
made after obtaining
his liberty from the Lilliputians

was for permission to visit the capital of their empire, the metropolis Mildendo, which lay a short distance – relatively speaking – from the beach where he had been tied. The sight of the city's towers in the not-too-distant distance, the puffs of smoke rising from ten thousand miniature chimneys aroused his curiosity. And, with passport in hand, Gulliver covered the distance between port and town in a couple of careful strides. ~ Sitting on a hillside overlooking Mildendo's walls, Man-Mountain surveys the scene: a model city whose architectural details are familiar in every respect, with the exception of their Lilliputian size. No doubt the view makes this onlooker feel as if he were somewhat out of sync and, no doubt, certain fears cloud his mind – for how will he fill his belly in a **Brobdingnag** world where a farm is no bigger than a flower bed and cattle stand four and a half inches high? But concerns over dislocation fade as he considers the advantages that his unique vantage provides: nearly two centuries before man learns to fly, Gulliver sees an entire city from the sky. In an instant, he grasps the logic of its overall design. ~ **BY DOUGLAS BLAU**

57

The New Urban Landscape
Exhibition catalog, 1989, offset lithograph
Designers: Stephen Doyle and Andrew Gray
Creative directors: Stephen Doyle
and William Drenttel
Firm: Drenttel Doyle Partners
Photographer (cover): Con Edison
Publisher: Olympia & York Companies (U.S.A.)
and Drenttel Doyle Partners, New York
Collection Cooper-Hewitt, National Design
Museum, Gift of Drenttel Doyle Partners

This catalog for an exhibition at the World Financial Center in New York borrows conventions from magazine design as well as from the classical tradition of the book. Each essay has a distinctive typographic treatment that comments on the text—a section on the city, for example, is organized as a typographic skyline. The classical device of opening a chapter with enlarged letters has been used to humorous effect by the designers, who have employed extreme shifts of scale to create a typographic interpretation of the text and photograph.

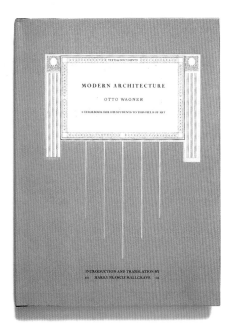

Modern Architecture
Book, 1988, offset lithograph
Designer: Laurie Haycock Makela (b. 1956)
Series design: Laurie Haycock Makela and Lorraine Wild
Publisher: Getty Center for the History of Art and the
Humanities, Santa Monica
Collection Cooper-Hewitt, National Design Museum,
Gift of Lorraine Wild

For this series of reprints of important works of
architectural theory, Laurie Haycock Makela and
Lorraine Wild created a format that allows each volume
to reflect the historical period and aesthetic content of
the text while maintaining a coherent identity for the
overall series. Historical ornaments and typefaces have
been used in a contemporary manner.

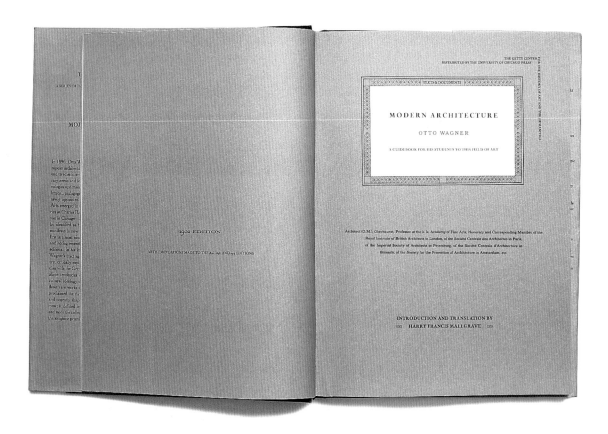

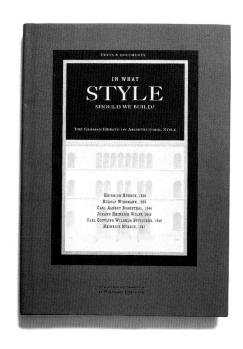

In What Style Should We Build?
Book cover, 1992, offset lithograph
Designer: Laurie Haycock Makela
Series design: Laurie Haycock Makela
and Lorraine Wild
Publisher: Getty Center for the History of Art
and the Humanities, Santa Monica
Collection Cooper-Hewitt, National Design
Museum, Gift of Lorraine Wild

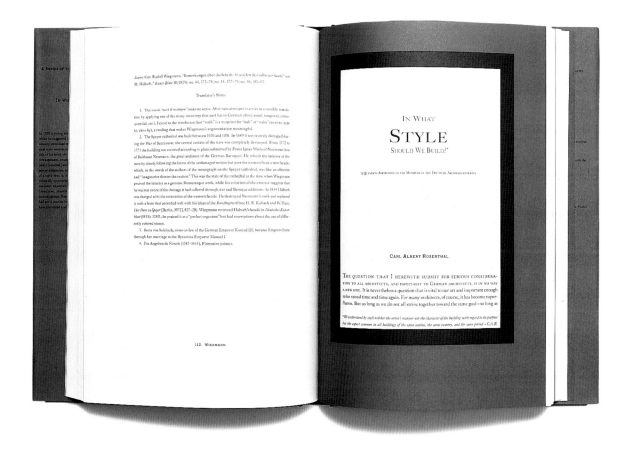

Martha Stewart Living
Magazine, 1995, offset lithograph
Designer: Anne Marie Midy (b. 1970)
Creative director: Gael Towey (b. 1952)
Art directors: Eric A. Pike, Agnethe Glatved,
Claudia Bruno, Constance Old, Scot Schy
Photographer: Victoria Pearson
Publisher: Time Publishing Ventures, Inc.,
New York

Martha Stewart Living (Peaches)
Magazine, July/August 1995, offset lithograph
Designer: Anne Marie Midy
Creative director: Gael Towey
Art directors: Eric A. Pike, Agnethe Glatved,
Claudia Bruno, Constance Old, Scot Schy
Photographer: Christopher Baker
Publisher: Time Publishing Ventures, Inc.,
New York

Martha Stewart Living (Ferns)
Magazine, 1995, offset lithograph
Designer: Anne Marie Midy
Creative director: Gael Towey
Art directors: Eric A. Pike, Agnethe Glatved,
Claudia Bruno, Constance Old, Scot Schy
Photographer: Margaret Roach
Publisher: Time Publishing Ventures, Inc.,
New York

The carefully staged photographs that are a
hallmark of *Martha Stewart Living* fit together into
luxurious mosaics. The Martha Stewart style has had
a broad impact on the housewares and gardening
industries, as seen in numerous consumer catalog
designs and the formats of competing magazines.

Home Garden
Magazine, 1995, offset lithograph
Designer and art director:
Brad Ruppert (b. 1965)
Photographer: Bill Holt
Publisher: Meredith Corporation,
Des Moines

The influence of *Martha Stewart
Living* can be seen in the format for
this gardening magazine.

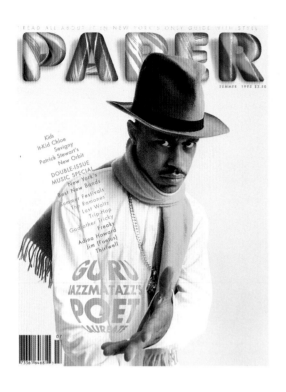

Paper
Magazine, 1995, offset lithograph
Art director: Bridget de Socio (b. 1960)
Photographer: Torkil Gudnason
Publisher: Paper Magazine
Publishing Inc., New York

Paper (Shades)
Magazine, 1995, offset lithograph
Art director: Bridget de Socio
Photographer: Marc Baptiste
Stylist: Stefan Campbell
Publisher: Paper Magazine
Publishing Inc., New York

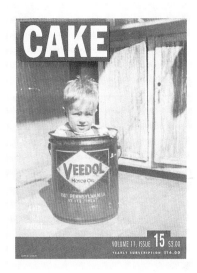

CAKE
Magazine, 1993, offset lithograph
Designer: Charles "Chank" Anderson
Publisher: CAKE, Minneapolis, Minnesota

FAD
Magazine cover, 1987, offset lithograph
Art and design: Richard Stutting (b. 1950)
Creative director: Dean Seven
Photographer: Doris Kloster
Publisher: FAD, San Francisco
Collection Cooper-Hewitt, National Design
Museum, Gift of Steven Heller

Spec
Magazine cover and spread, 1995,
offset lithograph
Designer and art director:
Martin Venezky (b. 1957)
Publisher: 24th Street Publishing,
San Francisco

Magazines of music and style are
published in cities across the country.
Such magazines stem from the
underground press of the 1960s.

Colors
Magazine, 1994, offset lithograph
Designers: Tibor Kalman and Paul Ritter
Photographer: Oliviero Toscani
Publisher: United Colors of Benetton

The global fashion company Benetton became famous in the late 1980s and 1990s for its ad campaigns, in which photographer Oliviero Toscani mixed representations of social conflict with the company's corporate image. The magazine *Colors* became a vehicle for exploring cultural issues in greater depth. In Tibor Kalman's format for the magazine, design and content are intimately linked. The essays are organized as collections of visual evidence annotated with multi-lingual captions. Each issue is printed in two languages, making the theme of cultural diversity an insistent presence on every page.

結局 違い は 何なの？ いろんな国のいろんな人に聞いてみた。

EUROPE ヨーロッパ

you live.

...ime being, I'm the only ...Hungary. The people

「今んとこ、ハンガリーじゃあ、
イボ族の子
なんて俺一人

ぐらいじゃないかなあ。だから仕事
場の連中も、
...me for
...ng an
...o.
　　皆、良くして
　　くれるよ。
最高さ」

ケネディ・マーチン
労働者
ブダペスト
ハンガリー

...'s really
...Kennedy
...worker,
...Hungary

「あたしセルビア人とスロバニア
人のハーフなの。だからクロアチア
の女の子から
...rbian and half Slovenian,
...rls in Croatia wanted to
けんかを
ふっかけられたわ。
この内乱

...nt with
...me.

...the war, it is
...be a Yugoslav
...via." –Tisana
...dent,
...Slovenia

の せいで、もうユーゴスラ
ビア人もユーゴスラビアっ
ていう見も、あったもんじゃ
ないわね」
ティサナ・ジナイチ
学生
ルビアナ、スロバニア

...yet experienced
人種差別
があるのは知ってるし
恐ろしい

...ad

...elf. But I know
...existence of
...ing, and I fear
...sence of skin-
...real threat. I
...st alone in the
...–Sunil Palikhe,
...g student,
...Hungary

と言うよね。内心穏やかじゃ
ないですよ。スキンヘッズ
の存在には本当におびえ
てしまう。夜の一人歩き
は絶対にしません」
スニール・パルケ
工学部学生
ブダペスト、ハンガリー

...od to fight my way
...schools as a Gypsy.
...problems, of course,
...d to live with them.
...to see my Gypsy chil-
...p, and to witness my
...en retain the
ジプシーとして成長

「ジプシーなので学校時代も苦労の
連続でしたが、それはそれで当たり
まえだと思います。問題はもちろんあっ
たけれど、対処の仕方を学びました
から、自分の子供たちも
我々の文化

をしっかり守り続けてくれ
ているのを見てるのは、本
当にいいもんですよ」
メセンット・ラカトス
作家
ペスト、ハンガリー
...ture
...people."
...Lakatos,
...apest.

NORTH AMERICA 北アメリカ

"I couldn't get my car started. A guy
kept hollering, 'You better
get back
on your side
of the river
where you belong.'
It was dark, time for me
to get back across the
river just like the guy told
me." –Debra Spindler, a
probation officer, Min-
neapolis, USA

「車のエンジンがなかなかかからな
いでいたら男が大声で怒鳴るの
よ。『川向こうのお前ら黒人の住み
かへ
さっさと
帰りやがれ』
って、日も暮れて暗くなっ
て来たから、確かにそいつ
の言ってるとおりに川の向
こうに戻ったほうが無難
な時間になっていたわ」
デボラ・スピンドラー
警官助観生
ミネアポリス、アメリカ

"That　　word 'albino' is a
slur.
It's used to single you out and
humiliate you. You hear it
yelled out of car windows.
So we like to 'peo-
ple with albinism.' I'm
a person with a condition,
not some kind of
a freak of nature."
–Matthew Smutko,
musician, New York,
USA

「『しらこ』って言い返事だ。
つまはじきにして
辱める
のに使われる。通り過ぎる車の窓から
この言葉を投げつけられたりする。
自分たちでは「白皮質」と言
うようにしているの。そうい
った健康状態にあるだけ
であって 奇形なんかじ
ゃないんだから」
マシュー・スマトコ
ミュージシャン
ニューヨーク
アメリカ

"Living in Minnesota, which is
mostly
white
people,
when your kids are
accepted, I think
that's the best thing
that can happen to
you." –Aurora Gavino,
registered nurse,
Minneapolis, USA

「ミネソタ州に住んでいて、せめて
自分の
子供たち
だけでも
受け入れてもらえたら、
もうそれだけで最高と思わ
なくちゃ」
オーロラ・ガビーノ
看護婦
ミネアポリス、アメリカ

"My girlfriend took me on a cruise
ship. All the employees were Fil-
ipinos or Hispanics and most
of the passengers were white.
I'm mestizo Colombian. Sometimes the passengers would ask
me to fix things in their cabins
because they
assumed
I was a janitor
or steward." –Miguel
Angel Varon, artist,
Los Angeles, USA

「ガールフレンドと豪華客船でクル
ーズに出かけたら、従業員は全員フ
ィリピン人かスペイン系で、おまけ
にお客はほとんど白人だった。僕は
コロンビア人で、スペイン人とイン
ディオのハーフなんだけど、他の客か
ら、他の客室の用事を何度も頼まれた。
掃除係か
給仕人
だと思われてたんだ」
ミグエル・エンジェル・
バロン
アーティスト
ロサンゼルス、アメリカ

ASIA アジア

"My first experience with my host
family was fantastic. They said that
they asked God to help them ac-
cept me as a person. I think that is
quite progressive for a Japanese.
I am sick of being considered
black
first
and foremost." –Lloyd
Walker, student, Kyoto, Japan

「ホーム・ステイの家族との初対面
ときたら本当に傑作だった。黒人を
人間扱いできるかどうか不安で神様
にお祈りしたそうだ。日本人のわり
には、すごく努力してるよね。でも、
真面目な話、いつも
黒い肌の
ことばかり
言われるのにはすっか
り嫌気がさしているんだ」
ロイド・ウォーカー
学生
京都、日本

"Of course people look at you as
though you are
an animal
or something. When I first came,
I really felt the prejudice. It's
true, people would say,
'Hey, you're a foreign-
er, you must have a
big dick.' Even in
restaurants it has
happened to me and
people just giggle
at me." –Michael
O'Day, clown,
Kyoto, Japan

「『動物か
何かのように
見られます。最初に来た時は
ひどく偏見があるのを感じたも
んです。『おい、外人、お
前チンコでかいだろう』
なんて言われるんど
とかでそういうこと
があっても、まわり
の人たちは笑ってい
るだけなんだ」
マイケル・オーティ
クラウン
京都、日本

"Usually in Japan I can't express
my opinion. I have to
kill my
feelings. I have to follow
everyone else even if I don't
like it. If I were black in the
USA I'd fight against discrimination. Although it's
true we also have a lot of
discrimination here."
–Hiromi Yoshida,
office clerk, Osaka,
Japan

「日本ではふつう自分の意見を言っ
たりはしないの。
感情を殺して
イヤでも
他の人たちと同じようにしてい
ないといけないの。もし私がア
メリカに住んでいる黒人だっ
たら差別と戦うと思うわ。
ここにも本当はものすごく
差別があるんだけれど....」
吉田弘美
事務員
大阪、日本

"There are many white people who don't like the
truth
and when we don't like it when we tell the truth.
That's how discrimination starts. The white people say they know everything, that they have
the knowledge to make machines, that they have
their technology. The whites say we are lazy;
we only sleep, eat and reproduce." –Davi
Kopenawa Yanomami (Yanomami Indian),
medicine man, Roraima, Brazil

「本当のことがお好きじゃない白人が大勢いらっしゃるん
だよね。私らが
本当のこと
を言ったりしたら、そりゃあ、お気に召さない。そ
うして人種差別が生まれるわけさ。自分らは何もか
も車知で機械をつくる知識も技術もお持ちだそう
だ。ひきかえ、私らはなまけ者で、食っちゃ寝して
子供ばっかり作ってると、言われるんだ」
ダヴィ・コペナワ・ヤノマミ（ヤノマミ族インティオ）
メディシン・マン（天然薬草調合師）
ロライマ、ブラジル

SOUTH AMERICA 南アメリカ

"I think things happen in extremes
to black people, either very good
or very bad. Even with all the discrimination, with police abusing
us, I am glad to be black. If I were
offered a pill to become white, I
would never take it. Mulatto,
maybe, but
never
white."
–Alexandre Coelho
Reis, office clerk, Rio
de Janeiro, Brazil

「黒人には極端なことばかり起きる
よね。すごーく良いことか、すごー
く悪いことかのどちらかだ。差別さ
れたり、警察に長暴されたり、それ
でも黒人で良かったと思う。飲んだ
ら白人になれる薬があったとしても
絶対に飲まないね。混血なら考えて
もいいけど
絶対白人
なんかに
なりたくない」
アレグザンドラ・
コーレホ・レイス
事務員
リオデジャネイロ
ブラジル

"I wouldn't want to be Indian or
black in Brazil. They are treated like
second-class
citizens.
Yet you always see blacks
smiling, singing, dancing
samba, even when they
don't have anything else in
life. How is that possible? I
wish they would teach me
their secret." –Zelia Moreira
de Souza, retired
teacher, Rio de
Janeiro, Brazil

「ブラジルのインティオや黒人にだ
けは決してなりたくないわ。まるで
二流市民
扱いですもの。なのに黒人たら、い
つ見ても、笑ったり歌ったりサン
バを踊ったりしてるの。他に
何もなくてもね。どうして
あきぐっていられるのか
しら。秘訣を教えてもら
いたいわ」
ゼリア・モレイラ・デ・
スーザ
元教師
リオデジャネイロ
ブラジル

"Once when I was looking for a
job as a dentist, I was hired immediately because I was 'Japanese.' The clinic didn't even check
with past employers or my
university. Brazilians
trust
Japanese more than
they do blacks and
even whites." –Vilma
Massae Haya-
kawa, dentist,
Rio de Janeiro,
Brazil

「歯科医の仕事を探していたら「日
系人」だということですぐに雇っ
てもらえたし、私の前の勤務先や学
校の照会もなかったんです。ブラジ
ル人は黒人や白人より
日系人のことを
断然信頼
してくれます」
ヴィルマ・マサエ・
ハヤカワ
歯科医
リオデジャネイロ
ブラジル

THIS APOLLO 11-SHAPED POCKETBOOK COMMEMORATED THE FIRST SUCCESSFUL MOON WALK, JULY 20, 1969.

dean
dick
stockwell

INTERVIEW *(Orbit)*
Magazine, 1990, offset lithograph
Art director: Fabien Baron (b. 1959)
Photographer: Albert Watson
Originally published in **INTERVIEW,**
Brant Publications, Inc., July 1990

INTERVIEW *(Dean Stockwell)*
Magazine, 1990, offset lithograph
Art director: Fabien Baron
Photographer: Fabrizio Ferri
Originally published in **INTERVIEW,**
Brant Publications, Inc., March 1990

INTERVIEW
Magazine, 1991, offset lithograph
Art director: Tibor Kalman (b. 1949)
Photographer: Kurt Marcus
Originally published in **INTERVIEW,**
Brant Publications, Inc., January 1991

The abstract typographic compositions that
Fabien Baron created for *Interview* in the late
1980s and early 1990s treated letterforms
as monumental objects. Tibor Kalman's work
for the same magazine rejected Baron's
formalism in favor of a language-based
approach. Kalman's typography actively
annotates the images, constructing an
interpretive scrim of parenthetical remarks.

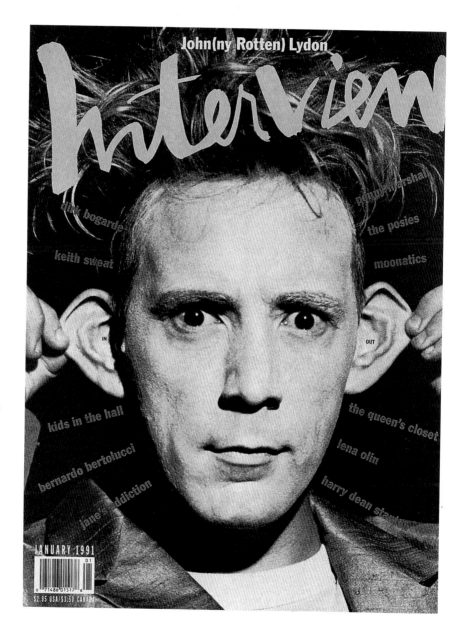

Panache
Magazine, 1980, photocopy
Designer and publisher:
Mick, York, United Kingdom

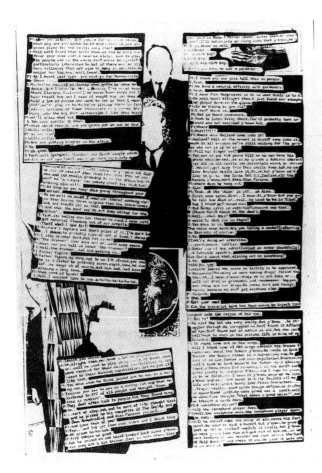

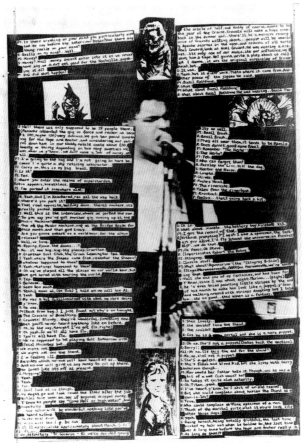

Open Magazine: Urban Control
Pamphlet, 1992, offset lithograph
Series editors: Greg Ruggiero and
Stuart Sahulka
Publisher: Open Media, Westfield,
New Jersey

Farm Pulp
Magazine, 1994, photocopy
Designer and publisher:
Gregory Hischak (b. 1960), Seattle

The current production of fanzines is rooted in the punk rock movement of the late 1970s, when magazines like *Panache*, published in the United Kingdom, were produced on photocopy machines and circulated among small circles of initiates. *Farm Pulp* is a contemporary journal celebrating masculine kitsch. The *Open Magazine* pamphlet series takes the fanzine genre in a more serious direction; each issue features a lecture or essay not easily available in other formats. The pamphlets are offered in book stores for a few dollars each.

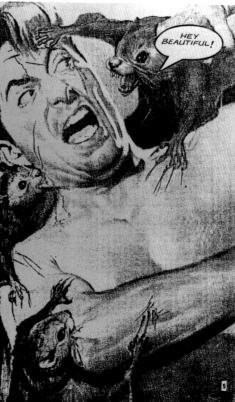

Nick Gorlin
The handsome Client Services Supervisor, he made client supervision his life—but now faces new kind of challenge, one that totally unexpected.

Tessa Cabot
Twenty-seven, beautiful, born to wealth, she was brought in to do of accounting—the beginning of desperate chapter of life, death. love.

David Cord
Charming, dedicated, he was th most likely to succeed Nick Go but Cord had a problem, and her was Emily.

SELECTED INTERVIEWS

WILLIAM DRENTTEL AND STEPHEN DOYLE
DRENTTEL DOYLE PARTNERS
New York, July 1996

Describe the design world in the 1980s.

SD: Not being a critic or reviewer, that's a question I can only answer from a personal perspective. The mid-1980s were a turning point for me—we started Drenttel Doyle Partners in June of 1985, smack in the middle of the decade, about same time that Apple launched the Macintosh. I had been at M&Co. for about two years. The design totems of the day were Milton Glaser, Ivan Chermayeff, Massimo Vignelli, and Pentagram.

WD: Don't forget that the mid-80s were boom years. An economic heyday coupled with a very optimistic business outlook spawned lots of ad agencies and design studios. I was at Saatchi & Saatchi, and we were mushrooming out of control, swallowing up other agencies. And there were a ton of start-ups, all paying high rent.

SD: This was the time when M&Co. was coming of age, getting attention for going against the prevailing flow of "good-taste" design. The design climate was heady, glossy, die-cut, and foil-stamped. At M&Co. the design idea took precedence over the flourish of the finish. The work was grubby-but-smart. It got people's attention. The idea was to allow things to be quirky, to let reason take a leave of absence, that certain flaws were more memorable and more personable than the smarmy majority of slick design being done. Remember all those real estate brochures?

WD: But another thing was going on, on a different level. The masters of the day were perfecting the structures of corporate identity: pure, perfectly organized, unassailable. The problem was that these attributes were focused on system over personality—and some corporations wanted both. Thrust Tibor Kalman into this void, and the story gets interesting. The buzz over M&Co. wasn't based on a huge body of work. The work itself had an uneasy relationship with the idea of the client—as if M&Co. were trying to turn all these systems inside out for the client's own good. Out of this conflict came some of their best work.

SD: As soon as it came to be expected, the prevailing good—which was great—wasn't good enough anymore, so the un-good of Tibor and his pranksters became the rage.

If you are describing a generational shift taking place, who represents the previous generation?

SD: Milton Glaser, once a rebel and iconoclast, seems to represent the reasonable parent, doesn't he? The calming godfather of design, and teacher of just about everybody.

Including you?

SD: Not only was he my teacher at The Cooper Union, but also my first boss at *Esquire* magazine. It was Milton's illustrations on the Shakespeare classics that got me interested in design in the first place, back in high school.

A lot of interesting people came out of The Cooper Union between the late 1970s and mid-1980s—you, Tom Kluepfel, Alexander Isley, Emily Oberman, and some others. What was the school's influence on you?

SD: My cathartic experience at Cooper, honestly, was being thrown out of the painting classes. Left with only design classes to choose from, I was amazed that the teachers weren't threatened by humor. Humor and personality and quirkiness were actually encouraged as devices of attention and tools of comminucation. This kind of thinking—from Rudy de Harak to Milton Glaser, Henry Wolf, Seymour Chwast, and Walter Bernard—culminated in George Sadek, head of the design program. He's the unsung instigator behind this off-kilter modern-classicism. Tom refers to George's genius as "lunacy over logic, within the context of literacy." It's those same ideas that we are still chasing today. We're interested in what words say before we're interested in how they look, but then we try to bring meaning and presentation together in a way that makes room for irony, humor, subterfuge, and surprise.

DAN FRIEDMAN
New York, June 1994

What do you think about the state of design today?
Is graphic design pervasive throughout society, or is it virtually non-existant? I've been asking this question for quite a long time, and I don't know how to answer it. We want people to be aware of what we do, aware of what makes it different and worthwhile, and yet we also want to be inclusive in our definition of "design"....

There's so much in-fighting among the members of the "edge"—a frenzy about originality. It reminds me of the stuff that would go on during the late 1960s and early 1970s. Wolfgang Weingart was infuriated that everyone was ripping him off. He was a spoiled brat, but I think he deserves the ultimate credit for the "new typography."

Describe the connection between you, April Greiman, and Wolfgang Weingart.
In a nutshell: I went to study in Ulm in 1967. I had gotten a Fulbright to go to Germany, even though I really wanted to go to Basel. I became fascinated with the theoretical approach at Ulm. At Basel, in 1968, they had just started the post-graduate program. I wanted to be in the first class. I was one of two Americans, and Weingart had just started teaching there. He was young—about my age. Our relationship was more as friends than as a student/teacher relationship. But it is important to say that I was influenced by him. He was reacting against rational Swiss typography, the work of the previous generation....

Unlike Weingart, I wasn't reacting *against* Swiss typography, because that rational system didn't really exist here in the United States except in isolated instances. Whereas Wolfgang Weingart was teaching based on intuition, I was trying to verbalize, demystify, the structures of typography. I wanted to create a method. I had to find a way to teach the rules and also how to break them at the same time, since nobody knew the rules.

When Wolfgang started lecturing and teaching in the United States in the early 1970s, he realized he needed to construct a methodology, too. I believe my work was a useful model for him in that respect....

In 1972, I was teaching one day a week at PCA [Philadelphia College of Art, now the University of the Arts], flying down to Philadelphia from New Haven. Louis Kahn and I took the same flight. That's when I met April....She had just come back from Switzerland, where she had studied for one year. She wasn't happy there, except in Weingart's classes. She had been aware of my work through Weingart, and we became friendly during the second semester at PCA. From the very beginning, I had discussions with her about her intuitive approach to typography. She was intuitive like Weingart. He had even done a cover of *TM* magazine with her picture on it, saying "I feel typography." I thought that was kind of corny.

Often, I would play devil's advocate with April, arguing for a more rigorous methodological approach, especially in teaching. April continues to work from an intuitive base, and, like Weingart, she has excellent intuitions. But I'm still hung up on content. She would say that there is content in the form. And I would say, yes, but it's a very limited means of expressing content. Consider minimalist painting, such as Albers: there is implicit meaning there. But that's a very narrow territory to work in. It limits the kind of content you can deal with.

I still follow April's work. She sees California as a place somewhere in outerspace, moved by primal spirits. I see it as a place where there are earthquakes, mudslides, and gang warfare. As she sees it, her "heavenly hyperspace" has meaning in it—Jungian psychology, spiritual issues— but to me it's limited in its ability to deal with other kinds of issues....It's hypocritical for me to criticize it too much, though, because I'm often guilty of the same thing. The difference is, I keep it in my own apartment.

STEFF GEISSBUHLER, PRINCIPAL
CHERMAYEFF & GEISMAR INC.
New York, June 1994

Describe your approach to corporate identity.
Over the years, we've come to approach identity in a different way. For example, for Knoll, we're focusing not on the logo but on an overall look and visual language. We've kept Massimo Vignelli's logo, because it's strong and has a history. We haven't approached the project in the old-fashioned sense of a trademark locked up with a typeface.

In the 1950s and 1960s, people working in corporate identity were discovering that repetition is important—the need to convey a consistent image. But that approach became too rigid, especially for smaller organizations, institutions, or companies that have other things to express—such as Knoll, where they want to express their creativity and attitude in presenting their design-intensive product.

Tell me about the work you did for Time Warner.
The Time Warner merger was a clash of cultures: Steven J. Ross, former chairman of Warner Communications, represented film, video, and television, while N. J. Nicholas, former chairman of Time Inc., represented serious journalism coming from a newspaper tradition. To represent the merger was very difficult. We showed them five different *TW* combinations, plus the eye and ear symbol. The products of both Time and Warner appeal to the eye and ear. But how do you combine an eye and an ear? It sounds good in theory, but it's difficult to do. Everyone said, You can't do another eye, because that's CBS. This town is not big enough for two eyes.

The eye/ear symbol was extremely well received by Steve Ross, who was the more flamboyant of the two chairmen. Ross convinced Nick that this was the way to go. Nicholas was very supportive and a great guy who knew that visual stuff was more Ross's territory.

We also proposed that the logo be purple to symbolize the merger—Time was traditionally associated with red, and Warner with blue. But purple wouldn't do—too "fruity" a color for Nicholas. Purple was okay for hairdressers, but not for these black-ink newspaper guys.

The designers of Warner's old logo had told them that their blue was "very special," and the designers of Time's logo had told them that their blue was "very special." It turned out that both companies were using exactly the same PMS color for their stationery—nothing special about it at all. We changed the color to a darker blue.

Why did Gerald Levin change the logo? New executives like to make their mark by changing logos—it's cheaper than changing the architecture, although it's still exorbitant. The explanation for switching to a neutral typographic treatment was that our symbol was too powerful an image, that it competed with the individual identities of Time Warner's many subsidiaries. The eye/ear symbol is still used by Time Warner Cable.

What's important in corporate identity right now?
Corporate identity consists of a complete visual language, not just a trademark. If it's well done, corporate identity can communicate a lot about the workings of a company. It can say a lot about how a business runs. But the most important function of corporate identity is to increase brand recognition. No advertising campaign works if people don't know who authored the ad. Brand recognition is the most important value of corporate identity for companies. Think of Xerox—the made-up company name with *x*'s on either end. It's become the generic name for photocopying and a whole class of office machines.

Executives have become more aware of graphic design, but business schools still don't teach the value of graphic design. In Switzerland, the situation is very different. Graphic design is part of the culture there—I never had to explain to my mother what a graphic designer is.

JONATHAN HOEFLER
New York, June 1996

What is your relationship to history?
A little like my relationship to gravity: truly inescapable. Most of the work for which I am known has a strong connection to history, at least insofar as history is represented through the history of typography. The historical precedents come through in varying degrees: a typeface like Mazarin, which is an explicit revival of a specific artifact (Jenson's type of 1470), obviously has more historical footing than a face like Ziggurat, which is a synthesis of an entire idiom (the nineteenth-century "egyptian"). I think *all* work has a connection to what has gone before, and that it's a twentieth-century conceit that typefaces can be designed outside the historical continuum.

What I find challenging is the investigation of historical styles and their expansion into new territories. Replicating an old font isn't as interesting as expanding on a historical theme. The Proteus Project is a family of typefaces I created for *Rolling Stone*. It's a sort of "theme and variations" built around nineteenth-century lines. The family takes the slab serif Ziggurat as its foundation, and plays out that structure across a variety of nineteenth-century styles. There's a sans serif Gothic, a wedge-seriffed Latin, and a chamfered Grecian. I left history behind with the italics, for which (in two cases, the Latin and the Grecian) there are no historical precedents. The project was less a matter of imitating historical styles, and more a question of examining historical motives. The ultimate result is a family of types with internal cohesion but an unpredictable level of historical fidelity.

None of this is to suggest that a typeface needs to be inspired by or rooted in historical forms. Some of the most fulfilling projects I've undertaken have been inspired by conceptual inquiries, rather than any affection for traditional forms. My hope is that someday I'll be able to reconcile these two extremes.

Describe the field of type design today.
The community of professional typeface designers working today is very small, although Fontographer seems to have brought all the world's graphic designers into the guild. This has brought some new voices into what might otherwise be a stagnant conversation. Although typography has traditionally had a strong backbone of scholarship, it has missed out on the critical discourses that graphic design brings to the field.

We do seem to be making progress now toward a canon of typographic critique. Part of it has to do with coming to grips with history, and recognizing how our work relates to convention. Jeffery Keedy, Barry Deck, Jonathan Barnbrook, and Miles Newlyn, none of whom would have been traditionally called "type designers," have contributed some thoughtful work that takes a distinct historical stance—albeit an ironic one, or an aggressive one.

Most of the typography of this century can be traced back to an approach taken up by William Morris in the closing years of the nineteenth century, an approach that involves looking to the past to retrieve something lost. Right now we're beginning to recognize that we've exhausted this approach, and are caught up in the rush to find something new.

What about history in graphic design more generally?
I came into graphic design through an affection for historical style, at least as reenacted by designers of the 1980s who appropriated it for their own ends. It was those handsome book covers in Constructivist and Secessionist lettering, which I found so seductive as a teenager, that got me into the field. They brought me into contact with design history, albeit through a circuitous route. That nebulous quality of a typeface that allows it to be both historically correct and visually fresh has a direct counterpart in graphic design. Graphic designers and type designers share the same responsibilities to history: to be part conservator and part harvester.

KENT HUNTER AND AUBREY BALKIND
FRANKFURT BALKIND PARTNERS
New York, July 1994

Do you think that annual reports have changed in the past fifteen years?

AB: I think *we* changed the nature of annual reports. Designers used to look at annual reports out of context, as if they existed in a world that only included annual reports. Everything was about design. But annual reports need to compete in the world with other media—TV, magazines. What matters is how they communicate, which includes how they're written as well as how they're designed. Most annual reports are written in corporatese—so you start with non-communication and then compound that problem with non-focused design. We start by asking, Who does this company want to be talking to? What preconceptions do they have about the company? How can we change those preconceptions?

KH: The *Why?* annual report we did for Time Warner in 1989 was a seminal piece. It actually was reviewed in the general press, including the *New York Times*. The *Times* had two quotes from designers who didn't like the piece, and a quote from a Wall Street guy who loved it. The radical thing here was the way we handled the charts and financial information in the back. In their previous report, this material occupied six dense, gray pages of text. We boiled it down to a dynamic double-page spread.

AB: The *Why?* annual report first stood out because of its color—that's where a lot of the shock lies. The company wanted to say, We're a new company on the leading edge.

KH: It was our idea to put "Why?" on the cover in one-inch letters, because that's the question everyone was asking. We answered the question with a series of icons—the eye, the ear, and so on. The combination of image and type created a new design language.

AB: Mixing type with illustrations was new—you see this now in a lot of annual reports, which are derived from what we did. Some of this stuff with charts and graphs had been in magazines like *Spy*.

Print is an interactive medium. We used icons and factoids throughout the book, playing games that people would have to figure out. If you have to work a little to get something, you will remember it longer. There are a lot of different levels of information, so people can read the report in a variety of ways.

KH: Steff Geissbuhler was working on his new logo for Time Warner at the same time as we were working on the *Why?* annual report. We didn't know what he was doing, but he came up with the eye and ear pictographic icon while we were working with the same ideas. The second report we did for Time Warner dealt with the idea of communication—from pictograms to hi-tech. This report came out in six different languages, because the company was approaching governments and corporations worldwide to find strategic partners.

AB: In our work for Time Warner, we took things from surf culture, fashion, and media, and we brought them into corporate communications. We don't claim to have invented anything new, but we brought these forms into a new place.

Richard Wurman has said that annual reports are obsolete. Do you think they will disappear?

AB: We think that annual reports *have* disappeared. Most annual reports now are vehicles for talking to employees or other audiences beyond the financial audience. Analysts aleady know the financial information they need to know—they're wired. They get it way before the report comes out.

But companies have to communicate—there's more need for that now rather than less. They have to communicate in order to exist. But how? Not necessarily in print. In a few years companies will have their own digital channels on-line, for communicating internally.

We've tried to use annual reports as a way to metamorphosize the company's identity from year to year. Corporate identity shouldn't be fixed. Most corporate identity systems are monolithic, like Russian communism. The only thing that works is democracy. You must allow room for counter-cultures in order to sustain the main culture. If an idea is strong, it should continually be challenged; otherwise it will die.

MARLENE McCARTY AND DONALD MOFFETT BUREAU

New York, June 1994

How did you come to found Bureau?

MM: Don and I met at Gran Fury, doing design together. We worked well together. I was already involved with Gran Fury when I went to work at M&Co. in 1987. At that time, they were working on some latter-day Talking Heads stuff, Florent ads, and so on. There was this "language of the vernacular" thing going on at M&Co. Suddenly, Tibor [Kalman] started this rhetoric about design being political. I feel, perhaps possessively, that this rhetoric was largely appropriated from Gran Fury.

At one point after Don and I had founded Bureau, Michael Bierut called me to interview me for an article he was writing. He wanted to find out if Gran Fury had evolved out of M&Co. I was personally outraged that this perception was out there, and I declined to participate in the article.

Don and I founded Bureau in late 1989.

Tibor Kalman has often said that there was the crap work at M&Co. and then the projects he really cared about. Is there a divide like that here at Bureau?

DM: I love doing the work for Clinique. Although it helps pay the bills, we don't treat it as a secondary project at all. We don't want to do uninteresting work. We try to keep boring projects from coming in the door at all.

MM: It's important to find ways to have fun doing all of the jobs we take on. It's a disaster if you don't enjoy working on a project—everyone comes out of the situation unhappy.

Where does your formal vocabulary come from?

MM: We just do what we can. I studied at the School of Design in Basel, where I learned a formalist approach to design. Deep in my heart, I trust that I can make anything turn out okay formally. There's no fear here about form.

DM: My background is art and biology.

MM: I have an ingrained formal ability—I can make it work. Don's more emotional—he says to "make it louder."

Are you treating the mass media as a vernacular? For example, in the Elektra ads, you use stock photographs and harsh gothic typography.

In Gran Fury we talked about the "authority of the media." Our idea was to use that authority to sell a different agenda. The Elektra ads aren't the best example, since that's a commercial message. But for all the theorizing I could do about design, it often comes down to "what we like." It's often just intuitive, blind faith. "I like the red letters better," and so on.

How do you connect your art practice and your design practice?

DM: We used to try to integrate them more. It's not that one contaminates the other....

MM: A lot of it has to do with economy. We both draw a salary from Bureau, which we didn't do at first. It's hard to define how you divide art time and Bureau time. The fairest thing is to say that the first eight hours are Bureau time. This causes its own problems—when do you do your art?

Maud Lavin did a piece in *Art in America* that "outed" me as a graphic designer. It was a great piece. We used to spend more time trying to make the two merge. But people need to categorize; they need to keep the two worlds separate. One group doesn't understand the other.

Are you interested in anything happening in graphic design right now?

DM: To be honest, no.

MM: There's a lot of nice-looking design going on, but there's so much more that interests me in the art world.

DM: Art and film are the areas that vitally interest us. Film is an art form I truly love.

MM: People hate art because it's boring, dead, and closed in on itself. And people just don't understand what graphic design is. It's devalued because it's ephemeral.

PAULA SCHER
New York, August 1995

What makes your typographic work distinct?
At Tyler School of Art in Philadelphia, we were taught the Swiss International Style of typography: Helvetica on a grid. I have very bad neatness skills, so that approach didn't work for me. I felt I was being forced to clean up my room. So I became an illustration major. I didn't really draw well, but when I came to New York to look for work, I found that my ideas were good. My teacher, the Polish designer Stanislav Zagorski, had told me to try illustrating with type. So I learned about type in relation to image.

At CBS Records, I would follow the content by echoing it with typography. I would copy a typographic genre and turn it into a record cover in relationship to the cover image. This was not atypical at the time. In the late 1970s there was an economic crash, and as an art director I could no longer afford to put all of our money into imagery. So the type came forward. My work was period influenced—the 1930s, Art Nouveau, Constructivism.

My biggest influence was Seymour [Chwast]. I met him in 1970 with my portfolio. We've married each other twice—once when I was 25, then again when I was 40. I responded to Push Pin when I was in school. They were my heroes. They combined illustration with typography, and they used letterforms from historical periods that I identified with. I was in art school from 1966 to 1970—I liked what was cool at the time, like any art student. Victor Moscoso and the Fillmore posters. I loved Victorian graphics and wood type. I still do.

Has your work changed since your years at CBS?
I have become less interested in rich, illustrative imagery. 90 percent of what I do is just type. Something happened in the 1980s. Clients started to interfere with the process—you would show them an illustration, and they would want to change it, and I found that embarrassing. Also, the illustrator always got the credit for the work. I feel more like the author if the project is typographic.

Describe your identity program for the Public Theater.
George C. Wolfe [the creative director] had clear, specific goals. The organization was intricately linked to Joseph Papp. To many people, it was the Joseph Papp Theater. The problem was, Joseph Papp had died. So people thought the theater must be dead, too. That's a big image problem. Paul Davis's posters were connected to Joseph Papp's image. Also, Davis's work was linked in people's minds with Masterpiece Theater. His posters were amazing, but we needed to start over to rebuild the image of the Public Theater. It was a tall order, because Paul Davis was loved so well. I felt I couldn't use illustration at all. I focused on type so that no one would compare the new work with that of Paul Davis. Then there was the problem that the New York Theater Festival was better known than the Public Theater as a total organization. We made "PUBLIC" big, so that people would know they were going to the Public.

Does the Public Theater identity draw on any historical or vernacular references?
The different scale relationships coupled with stamps come from Dada. The Apollo Theater posters are another source. They were done in wood type on silkscreened grounds of gradated color. Instead of letterspacing to make everything fit, the printer changed the size of the letters. What they wouldn't do, though, is change the axis of some of the words, as I have done in the Public Theater work.

George Wolfe once told me that at the Public Theater he wanted to make elite culture popular and popular culture elite. That's what I want to do with graphic design.

I've always been what you would call a "pop" designer. I wanted to make things that the public could relate to and understand, while raising expectations about what the "mainstream" can be. My goal is not to be so above my audience that they can't reach it. If I'm doing a cover for a record, I want to sell the record. I would rather be the Beatles than Philip Glass.

LORRAINE WILD
Los Angeles, July 1994

The fact that you have studied at both Yale and Cranbrook, and have taught at CalArts and directed the program there, gives you a unique perspective on theory and graphic design.

The big story in design education since around 1984 or 1985 has been the reworking of the design curriculum. There has been a movement away from two main tracks: commercial formalism and the straightforward modernist program. In the graduate program at CalArts, Edward Fella, Jeffery Keedy, and I handle theory—as part of the studio projects—in a non-academic way. The first project we do in the first year is called *The Lexicon*. We start with words that are used to describe literary as well as visual form— "metaphor," "ambiguity," and so on. Students research the meaning and use of these terms. The project immediately sets the tone that we're going to look at everything in verbal as well as visual terms.

CalArts has a great humanities and art history/theory faculty. We encourage our students to go to these other faculty members to broaden their perspectives beyond the confines of the studio. We're trying to demystify the notion that the designer's point of view is the sole source of meaning. We hope that connections made outside of the studio will lead designers to a greater understanding of both what they know and what they do not know. This understanding will enable more productive collaborations and partnerships, which seems critical for future practice.

This is very different from how I was trained at Yale in the early 1980s. I was never asked to consider that what I was making might be read in a different way than I had intended. In fact, I don't remember being asked to consider that my work would be read at all. Meanwhile, amazing stuff was happening in the Department of Comparative Literature—Umberto Eco and others were teaching at Yale at the time—yet students would be criticized if they took "too many" non-studio courses.

How do you think theory and design should interact?

One thing I don't like in art and design education is to watch design teachers try to present critical theory in a diluted way. Designers should be able to use theory, but they should understand the nature of their own interpretations of theory (and see them as that—interpretations). Theory has opened up a multitude of ways that we can understand our work, but it will not tell anyone how to produce better or more interesting design. Graphic design will continue to be measured—or seen—through its visual manifestations, in all their variety.

Some of the curricula now being developed acknowledge that design has a past. At the same time, technology is pushing teachers and students to think about the future, to imagine practices that are radically different from the print-based, analog past.

I suppose the conditions I am describing explain my continuing fascination with modernism right before and after World War II (after the avant-garde of the 1920s and before the codification of the 1950s). At that time, design was understood to be primarily conceptual, subject to a variety of visual interpretations. Designers working at the Chicago Bauhaus and Black Mountain College were proceeding optimistically in a period of great uncertainty.

So, unlike earlier educators, we are not looking for a set of universal rules, but we, too, have to talk about methods that will help students work through a future that can't be accurately predicted. This new element in the curriculum—theory—is what rattles practitioners who think that the "blue sky" experimentation of design schools doesn't apply to the problems of practice, and yet these designers are out there every day facing the same momentous changes. Though the realms of design education and design practice seem very far apart, we are probably closer now, in terms of the conceptual problems confronting all of us, than we've been in a long while.

BOOK DESIGN
Ellen Lupton

COVER DESIGN
Chip Kidd

EDITOR
PRINCETON ARCHITECTURAL PRESS
Mark Lamster

EDITOR
NATIONAL DESIGN MUSEUM
Kathleen Luhrs

DIRECTOR OF RESEARCH
Paul Makovsky

MANAGING EDITOR
Timothy McCormick

TYPOGRAPHY
Interstate Family
Designed by Tobias Frere-Jones
Courtesy Font Bureau, Boston

PRINCIPLE PHOTOGRAPHERS
Matt Flynn
John Halpern
Ken Pelka

PHOTO CREDITS

MATT FLYNN
p 14, *Do You Love...*; p 18, *Dance Month*; p 22, *New*; p 24, all photos; p 25, all photos except *Republican Contract on America*; p 27, all photos; p 33, *Polvo*; p 38, *Avant Garde, Americana Alphabets*; p 40-44, all photos; p 46, *Stadttheater*; p 48, *Kreative*; p 49, *Vertigo*; p 53, *Fact Twenty Two*; p 56, *Lift and Separate*; p 59, all photos; p 62, *American Type Corp.*; p 64-67, all photos; p 68, *A New Wave...*; p 69, *Graves*; p 73-75, all photos; p 82, all photos; p 85, all photos; p 90, *Harley-Davidson*; p 93, *LACE*; p 94, all photos; p 96-97, all photos; p 100, all photos; p 106, all photos; p 108, all photos; p 110, *Modern Dog*; p 112, *Skolos/Wedell*; p 116, all photos; p 118, *Biography*; p 119, all photos; p 140-143, all photos.

KEVIN DOWNS
p 121, all photos; p 147, *Strange Attractors*.

JOHN HALPERN
p 45, all photos; p 79, spread from *Enter*; p 115, *Zone 3*; p 118, *The Castle, History of Luminous Motion, City of Boys*; p 122-123, all photos; p 124, *Ordonnance*; p 144-145, all photos; p 146, all photos; p 147, *Problems and Solutions*; p 148, all photos; p 152-155, all photos.

KEN PELKA
p 18, *Fantera, Killdozer, Spray Can, Uncensored...*; p 21, *Swoon*; p 22, *Rocket from the Crypt*; p 23, *Man of the Moment*; p 28, all photos; p 51-52, all photos; p 56, *Dazed and Confused*; p 57, all photos; p 69, *Cranbrook Architecture*; p 70-71, all photos; p 102, all photos; p 104, *WAC is Watching*; p 107, *Amazing New Ideas*.

All other photos were provided by the designers or scanned from printed proofs.

Photographs of objects donated to the National Design Museum by Tibor Kalman/M&Co. are copyright Tibor Kalman.